# GOD
## in the
# *Whirlwind*

# GOD
## in the
# *Whirlwind*

Stories of Grace from the
Tornado at Union University

Tim Ellsworth
*photography by Morris Abernathy*

B&H
PUBLISHING GROUP
Nashville, Tennessee

978-0-8054-4847-4


Published by B&H Publishing Group,
Nashville, Tennessee


Dewey Decimal Classification: 231.5
Subject Heading: PROVIDENCE AND GOVERNMENT OF
GOD \ TORNADOES—TENNESSEE \ UNION UNIVERSITY

All Scripture quotations are taken from the Holman Christian
Standard Bible®. Copyright© 1999, 2000, 2002, 2003 by Holman
Bible Publishers. Used by permission. Holman Christian Standard
Bible®, Holman CSB®, and HCSB® are federally registered trade-
marks of Holman Bible Publishers.

1 2 3 4 5 6 7 8 • 11 10 09 08

To Sarah:
My treasure and my love.
You are a daily reminder of God's smile upon me.
(James 1:17)

# CONTENTS

Foreword ix

Introduction 1

Kevin Furniss: A Hand of Life 11

Julie Boyer: A Prayer of Desperation 19

Danny Song: A Sofa of Shelter 27

Chris Lean: A Story of Conversion 35

Cheryl Propst: A Board of Protection 43

David Wilson: A Testimony of Grace 49

Candace Cross/Eric Smith: A Ring of Devotion 57

Aaron Gilbert: A Memorial of Mercy 65

Sarah Santiago: A Trail of Blood 73

Kimberly Thornbury: A Master of Preparation 79

Matt Taylor: A God of Control 85

Heather Martin: A Tub of Entrapment 91

Mark and Annie Wilson: A Journey of Uncertainty 97

Jasmine Huang: A Door of Communication 105

Mario Cobo: A Sense of Relief 113

Tori Gill: A Pleading of Relief 119

George Guthrie: A Ministry of Care 127

Blake Waggoner: A Symbol of Heroism 135

Julie Mitchell: A Hope of Rescue 141

David Dockery: A Pillar of Strength 145

Conclusion 153

Afterword 157

Acknowledgments 161

# FOREWORD

Christians have historically confessed that God as Father reigns with providential care over His universe, His creatures, and the flow of the stream of human history according to the purposes of His grace. The providence of God provides the best framework for interpreting the events associated with the tornado that devastated large portions of the Union University campus on February 5, 2008. The stories that are so powerfully told in this significant volume that you hold in your hands point over and over again to God's gracious providence.

My life, like so many others across the Union campus, will never be the same on this side of February 5. The events of that night will be etched in my memory for years and years to come. I will never forget the eerie darkness, the loud sound of the swirling tornado, the initial phone call telling me that portions of the campus had been hit, the first impressions after seeing the walls crumbling in the residence life area, the look on the faces of shocked students, and the amazing efforts of the rescue workers and those involved that night in the initial response. But most of all, I will never forget the sense of thanksgiving to God that I experienced that night upon learning that all of our students were alive. Yes, some were seriously injured, but none were without hope.

Wednesday morning, February 6, we had the amazing privilege to tell the world of our confidence in God's providence and our trust in His grace as interview opportunities developed with international, national, regional, and local media, including television, radio, and print. Devastation was all around, but there was no despair. The words of the apostle Paul in 2 Corinthians 4 became our own. We were given a new way to see what had taken place on the Union campus. Our eyes were opened afresh. A work of God was beginning to take place. We began to pray that out of the rubble, God would bring renewal across our campus.

The initial assessments suggested that there had been nearly $40 million in damages to the campus. How could we respond to such devastation? How would we respond to this impending emergency? We were driven to a new and fresh dependence on God and His marvelous providence. We began to move forward, in light of this providential framework, to outline a plan to help guide us through the next few days and weeks.

Amazingly we were able to gather together on campus as a community exactly two weeks later (February 19) in a standing-room-only worship service in our chapel. We lifted our voices in praise and bowed our hearts in prayer, recognizing anew our deep dependence on God. The fourteen days between February 5 and February 19 were some of the most demanding and challenging that any of us have ever faced. Our faculty, staff, and students came together as volunteers to do whatever they could to help with the initial recovery efforts, including the retrieval of student belongings from the dorms. The diligent efforts of our trustees, administrators, faculty, staff, and students working together across the campus have been a joy to behold.

Classes were able to begin again on February 20, yet, things have been anything but normal. The spring schedule has been revised by Union's gifted and creative academic leadership. Numerous classes have had to be rescheduled in various places around the city. More than eight hundred students have now been relocated from the residence life area that has now been demolished.

We played our first home basketball game in front of a packed house on Thursday, February 21. The next day we held a forward-looking and hope-filled groundbreaking for fourteen new residence life complexes. We are grateful for God's grace to us over these past days as we have moved from those early hours of crisis to a time of rebuilding. While we have a lengthy and challenging road in front of us, we certainly have much for which to be grateful.

The new residential life project is now moving forward. We all pray for God's blessings on this important project. The repair work on all of the other buildings has also started. We have four contractors and numerous subcontractors at work on campus led by a single architectural and engineering firm. Each day seems busier than the day before. We find ourselves in unchartered waters functioning in an "essentialist mode," but we are pressing on with hopefulness in God's good providence, with an assurance that the same providential God who protected our students on the evening of February 5 will provide for us and guide us in this new journey.

This volume, over and over again through the eyes of people who experienced the storm in various ways, tells the inspiring stories of hope and trust in our providential God. *Hope* is a powerful word— a driving force in life. Hope includes a desire for something, but it is even more than that. It is an eager, confident expectation that sustains us while we work diligently and wait patiently. Hope is not escapism but is an energizing motivation for faithful living in the here and now. In the midst of our many challenges, hope stabilizes our lives, serving as an anchor to link us to God's faithful providence. We often sing about such hope: "O God, our help in ages past, our hope for years to come." Hope shapes and directs our service and gives it motivation so that while we wait and watch, we work faithfully.

The hope that will carry us forward is not self-reliant motivation, but a confidence in a God who intervenes in the affairs of human history. Without such a trust in our majestic Triune God, we would find the current challenges insurmountable. As a university community we are taking the next steps forward with the full recognition that God's providence transcends the experiences of men and women. In so doing, God can take actions that seem bad and use them for His good (see Gen. 50:20).

Such work on the part of God brings about a response of praise from believers for God's greatness. This book, so carefully compiled and edited by Tim Ellsworth, is just that: a book of praise. The book does not attempt to answer many unresolved and lingering questions with which we continue to struggle. Yet, it does point us to an infinitely powerful and absolute loving God. Somehow, in ways that we will understand in future days, the events associated with the devastating tornado that hit Union University on February 5 help us see that God has a plan and purpose for all things. This confession helps us put life in perspective (see Eccles. 9:11). We recognize that bad things happen. We acknowledge the huge and unexpected challenges that we now face. But we move forward in hope with assurance that our great God can and does use events for His eternal good, even events that are hard for us to fully understand.

The ultimate example is the crucifixion of Christ, which pictures Christ in His suffering state because of the sinful, evil actions of humanity. Yet through the triumph of the Resurrection, the worst act in history, the crucifixion of the God-Man Jesus Christ, became the greatest good, the provision for the forgiveness of sin, and the salvation of humankind. All of this points to God's wise and wonderful plan for this world, part of which has been revealed to us but which is finally incomprehensible in its totality to God's creatures. While we struggle with the injuries to Union students and the $40 million of damage to the Union University campus, we are reminded both as individuals and as a community, as told in such moving ways in this book, that our hope rests in God's wise and wonderful plan. Because of our hope in this God we do not lose heart (see 2 Cor. 4:1, 16–18). Our prayer as we move beyond February 5 is best expressed by the hymn writer, Henry Lyle (1793–1847), who wrote "Abide with Me":

> *Abide with me: fast falls the eventide;*
> *The darkness deepens; Lord with me abide:*
> *When other helpers fail, and comforts flee,*
> *Help of the helpless, O abide with me!*
>
> *Swift to its close ebbs out life's little day;*
> *Earth's joys grow dim, its glories pass away;*
> *Change and decay in all around I see:*
> *O Thou who changest not, abide with me!*
>
> *I need Thy presence every passing hour;*
> *What but Thy grace can foil the tempter's power?*
> *Who like Thyself my guide and stay can be?*
> *Thro' cloud and sunshine, O abide with me!*
>
> *Hold Thou Thy cross before my closing eyes;*
> *Shine thro' the gloom, and point me to the skies:*
> *Heav'n's morning breaks and earth's vain shadows flee:*
> *In life, in death, O Lord, abide with me!*

I am deeply grateful to Tim Ellsworth for his capable oversight of this project. I trust readers of this book will also find the sense of hope and renewal so beautifully reflected in the pages that follow.

—David S. Dockery
President, Union University
Easter, 2008

# INTRODUCTION

*"His path is in the whirlwind and storm, and clouds are
the dust beneath His feet." (Nahum 1:3)*

One stormy February night, the world showed up at our back-
door. The circumstances were not of our choosing, but suddenly
Union University in Jackson, Tennessee, was thrust into the international spotlight.

The original story itself was the stuff of headlines. A powerful
EF–4 tornado—with winds in excess of 200 miles per hour—slams
a university campus, causing $40 million in damage. It destroys eigh-
teen college dormitory buildings, leaving sixteen students trapped in
heaping piles of rubble. Rescue workers labor for five hours, through
predictions of a second destructive storm system, until the last person
is freed. Fifty-one students go to the hospital with injuries.

Nobody dies.

The disaster at Union University in Jackson, Tennessee, quickly
made news around the world, as TV crews from all over the country
flocked to Jackson to tell the story. CNN, FOX News, Good Morning
America, The Today Show, MSNBC, The Early Show, affiliates from
Boston, Nashville, Memphis, St. Louis—among many others—were
on campus to cover the events of February 5.

Charles Fowler, Union's senior vice president for university relations, was in Thailand when the tornado came through and watched
the story unfolding as he sat in an airport in Bangkok. He later saw
more stories in the Tokyo airport.

"It was just about the only story that was running on all the
news channels over there," Fowler said. "There was David Dockery
and Union University on CNN International, on BBC, and on Asian

1

channels as well. The first report I actually heard was on a British television station that was being broadcast in Thailand."

Reporters covering the story saw the extent of the damage. They saw the buildings lying in ruins. They saw the cars tossed hither and yon across the entire campus. And they marveled at the fact that nobody was killed.

Those of us at Union marveled, too. But we most likely came to a radically different conclusion than that of the media members who swarmed our campus. To most of us in the Union community, there was only one logical conclusion—God's providential protection was the reason nobody died. It was simply staggering to see the devastation and wonder how everyone got out alive. As the night's events unfolded, we weren't always sure that was going to be the case.

Union University Provost Carla Sanderson was at the hospital that night, monitoring the status of the students as they were rescued from the crumbled buildings and brought to the emergency room.

"We kept a concerned and watchful eye on those doors where the rescued would enter," Sanderson said. "I will never forget—never—the feeling, when around 1 a.m. Jason Kaspar was brought in through those doors. And he raised his hand and gave us a wave."

Not until then was Sanderson able to take her first deep breath since 7:02 p.m., when the tornado hit.

"God had been merciful and saved these lives," Sanderson said. "It was obvious some surgeries and ICU admissions were forthcoming, but every single student was awake and responsive, every one had some degree of movement and sensation in every limb, nothing was going to be permanent. It was then that the tears came. Those boys were all going to be OK."

Not only should people have died in the wreckage—dozens, if not hundreds, of people should have died. In fact, when firemen first arrived on the scene and saw the massive destruction, they notified the local hospital to prepare for one hundred deaths.

For some reason, however, God in His sovereignty delighted to spare us. No, He didn't spare everyone elsewhere. Dozens of people died from the tornado's blast in Tennessee and surrounding states. But He did protect us. We don't know why. We just know that He did.

Maybe God knew how Union University students would respond to His protection. One of the most encouraging e-mails I received in the days immediately following the tornado came from Fred Shackleford, a pastor in Paris, Tennessee. One of his church members had sent him this message:

"What a compliment to the Union students! I think God looked the world over and said, 'Here are some kids who will demonstrate their faith and speak for Me to the world. I will give them a platform of national TV to speak of faith and My unlimited grace and power.'"

Could that have been one of God's purposes for the way in which He delivered our students? Maybe so. But since we're not privy to the mind of God on such matters, any such surmising would only be conjecture. You'll have to come to your own conclusions. All we know for sure is that God protected the lives of everyone on campus, and for that He deserves our praise and gratitude.

Following the tornado's sweep through campus, the story at Union continued to gather steam for a few more days. Tennessee Governor Phil Bredesen and Homeland Security Secretary Michael Chertoff even visited Union to see the destruction for themselves.

Many of us at Union had been talking in recent months about ways we could increase the university's national profile. This wasn't what we had in mind—but as the news and media relations director for the university, I had all the news coverage I could have desired. Union had been the subject of more than four thousand newspaper articles and two thousand television broadcasts around the world by the time things finally settled down. Our story had appeared in almost every major metropolitan newspaper and on every TV network in the country. The blogosphere was abuzz with the reports. Some technology folks cited Union as an example of what organizational communication should be in a time of crisis. ESPN did a major story about our women's basketball team and the tornado.

Throughout the ordeal, the Union student body was a collective finger pointing to Christ. Consider just a few examples:

- On NBC's TODAY Show, sophomore Sarah Logan said, "We just felt God's hand of protection over us. When you look at the desolation and destruction on our campus and realize there were 1,200 students here and not one single fatality, you can't help but say that is a miracle and God was here protecting us."
- On CNN, senior Aaron Gilbert said, "We really felt the hand of God. One thing I noticed is where all the people were trapped,

there were little pockets keeping anything from harming them
or falling on them. It was definitely the grace of God."

• On FOX News, senior Claire Hamilton said, "At the time,
  I was just so calm. God just really calmed my nerves. We were
  so thankful to be alive afterwards."

• In the *Los Angeles Times*, freshman Amber Campagna said,
  "I know God kept everyone at this school safe. I don't know
  why God let it happen, but I really believe He was testing
  every student here."

• In the *Tennessean*, senior Candace Cross said, "I realized that
  I am not in control. I realized that Christ is totally in control.
  He protected each and every one of us."

• In the Florida *Fort Pierce Tribune*, sophomore Alyssa Bantz
  said, "There's really no physical explanation why we weren't
  killed. It really was God's hand over us. It was like God put
  bubble wrap for protection over us. He didn't protect all the
  structures in one big bubble, but every single spot where there
  was a student, He had his hand over."

This is only a small sampling of the kind of quotes you could
find from Union students in reports and articles all over the world.
Even while he sat in the airport in Bangkok, Fowler met a couple who
asked him where he was from. When he told them he was from Union
University, "Their first comments were, 'We saw on the television
that your school has been hit by a tornado. We have never been more
impressed with students as we have been in listening to your students'
testimonies,'" Fowler said.

In addition, there was the consistent testimony of Union University
President David S. Dockery, who was quoted countless times in the
media as saying similar things to what he told Memphis' *Commercial
Appeal*: "As painful as this is, it has united the Union community
in new ways and deepened our sense of shared identity and purpose.
I can't begin to describe all we're experiencing, but I can point to the
overwhelming grace and goodness of our God."

In short, God made much of Himself and His providence through
this ordeal, and it pleased Him to use Union University to do it.

In his book *The Mystery of Providence*, Puritan John Flavel
writes:

> If the admirable adaptation of the means and
> instruments employed for mercy to the people of God

are carefully considered, who can but confess that
as there are tools of all sorts and sizes in the shop of
Providence, so there is a most skilful hand that uses
them, and that they could no more produce such effects
of themselves than the axe, saw, or chisel can cut or
carve a rough log into a beautiful figure without the
hand of a skilful artificer?[1]

For Union students that night, God used tools like couches and
gumball machines, 2-by-4s and chainsaws, firemen and bathtubs, to
preserve life. He was most certainly a skillful artificer, a master com-
poser, who orchestrated all things perfectly—even, as you'll see in the
stories to follow, down to the very inch.

In the days after the storm, we talked quite a bit on campus about
the Union spirit, which triumphed through the despair and challenged
us to keep going. As Dr. Dockery astutely observed just hours after the
tornado's blast, "We've lost the buildings, but we haven't lost the spirit
of Union University, and that's what will carry us forward."

Indeed, it did.

When the campus lay in ruins, the Union community burst into
action. Administrators, faculty, staff, students, and community volunteers alike worked long hours to salvage as many of the students'
belongings as they could. They picked up debris, cleared away storm-
tossed cars, and found ways to make university life at Union work
again.

On February 19 the Union community gathered on campus for
a worship service in the G.M. Savage Memorial Chapel. That service
proved to be one of the most significant and most moving events in
the history of Union University. The next day, just two weeks after the
tornado that wiped away 70 percent of our campus housing, rendered
one academic building entirely unusable, and turned the Union parking lot into a giant salvage yard, classes began again. Few believed
it could be done. But with wisdom and guidance from God, Union's
academic leaders shifted schedules, moved offices, changed classroom
locations, and found a way to pull it off. This accomplishment was
as much God's work as His protection for the students during the
storm was. Most assuredly, we can do all things through Christ who
strengthens us.

But make no mistake. This "Union spirit" is not some mystical,
undefined abstraction that gives us all a glow and makes us feel warm

inside. It's not some nebulous impulse of confidence in our own abilities and sheer determination in the face of seemingly insurmountable
obstacles. Not at all.

Rather, the Union spirit is a confidence in the sovereignty and
providence of a gracious God who has protected us thus far. It is
faith in the redeeming sacrifice of Jesus Christ, and a hope that God's
purposes will be accomplished through us for His glory. That is what
binds us and makes us a union.

That is why we pulled together in a spirit of cooperation and
community—because we are brothers and sisters in Christ who have
a united interest in God being glorified above all. That is why our
students risked their lives to pull their friends from the wreckage of
shattered dormitories. That is why our students—unprompted and
unscripted—boldly testified before millions of people on international
television about their faith in God and His protection over them. That
is why they gladly pitched in and worked hard to help clean up after
the storm. That is why they were flexible and gracious in accepting
accommodations and arrangements that were less than convenient.
That is why Union is indeed a grace-filled academic community, as
Dr. Dockery likes to describe it.

But the main intent of this book is not to sing the praises of Union
University. Nor is this book intended to be an exhaustive chronicling
of the events surrounding February 5 and the days thereafter. It doesn't
tell the story of so many Union administrators, faculty, staff, trustees,
students, and friends who have given of their time and supported the
university in so many ways.

Instead, the stories included here are designed to exalt and mag-
nify the God who sheltered our students under His wing. They are but
a small window into the larger Union community, and a sampling of
God's amazing grace in the life of Union University.

In the pages to follow, you'll read stories about how the tornado
of February 5, 2008, affected all kinds of people at Union in all kinds
of ways. Some of them are stories of miraculous protection—of the
difference between life and death being a matter of mere inches. Some
of them are stories about how the tornado led to God working in the
lives of lost friends and family members and bringing them to faith in
Christ. All of them are stories about how God has changed lives and
acted providentially in the affairs of Union University.

To quote from Flavel again in *The Mystery of Providence*:

> If Christians in reading the Scriptures would judiciously collect and record the providences they shall meet with there, and (if destitute of other helps) but add those that have fallen out in their own time and experience, O what a precious treasure would these make! What an antidote would it be to their souls against the spreading atheism of these days, and satisfy them beyond what many other arguments can do, that "The Lord he is the God; the Lord he is the God" (1 Kings 18:39).[2]

The stories to follow are those that have fallen out in our time and experience. And what a treasure of God's grace they are.

Taken by themselves, these testimonies don't necessarily mean that much. Lots of people invoke God's name during times of trial and difficulty. Lots of people pour into churches the next Sunday after disaster, confronted afresh with their own mortality and the fragility of their lives.

But taken collectively, these testimonies do communicate the reality of Christ's pre-eminence at Union University. The accounts you'll find here aren't simply survivor stories. They are stories of faith in the midst of the tornado. They are stories of how God had His way in the whirlwind and storm. And they are potent examples of how a loving God protected the helpless, and used imperfect, sinful people to showcase His miraculous power and His saving grace to the entire world.

## Notes

1. John Flavel, *The Mystery of Providence* (Banner of Truth edition, 1963).
2. Ibid.

# Autumn Baldock

Freshman, Chemistry major from Memphis, Tennessee

*We sat and waited and waited, and finally thought nothing was going to happen so we all got up and went to look out the window of the bedroom beside the bathroom to see if we could see anything. When we opened the blinds, we saw the funnel coming straight towards us.*

*Next thing I know, I am surrounded by this blue and green light as I screamed. All of us got pushed back into the bathroom and thrown into the tub and the wall and the shelves outside the bathroom. I landed half in the bathroom, half in the hallway. It sounded like a hundred freight trains on top of us. The pressure was so bad it felt like someone was taking two bricks and squeezing my head between them.*

*My body felt like it was going to explode as it was being forced to the ground. Then it felt like my body was trying to be lifted from the ground. As I held on to the door frame of the bathroom, I truly thought I was going to die right there on that floor, surrounded by my friends. I thought for sure, I was going to see Jesus that night.*

*The next day, they let us near the dorm rooms and I saw nothing. Where my room used to be, there was nothing. Not a wall, or a roof, or a floor. Just a pile of rubble was all that was left. The staircase that used to lead to my front door, led to nothing.*

*Union is a special place, and maybe the only place where this could happen and God still get the glory. He spared every single soul on that campus that night in order that they may share their faith and His name throughout the world. I was holding God's hand that night and truly felt His arms encompass me as I cried out to Him in the darkness.*

# KEVIN FURNISS:
# A HAND OF LIFE

Junior, Bartlett, Tennessee

*"For I know the plans I have for you"—this is the LORD's
declaration—"plans for your welfare, not for disaster,
to give you a future and a hope." (Jeremiah 29:11)*

The most frightening night of Kevin Furniss' life began in the Watters
commons on the Union University campus, where the twenty-year-
old was playing ping pong with friends.

Kevin and six of his buddies were in the commons riding out the
storm that raged around them. Furniss, a Christian studies major,
decided to run back to his room to get his wallet, and by the time he
returned to the commons, the tornado was upon him. He raced into
the men's bathroom in the commons—the designated shelter area in
times of severe weather. Three of his friends were hunkered down
in that bathroom, with another three friends taking shelter in the
women's bathroom right next to the men's.

"I don't remember anything from there until it was on top of us,"
Furniss recalled. "I don't remember who was behind me or how we got
in the door or anything like that. It all happened and then everything
was on top of us."

By "everything" Furniss means the entire commons building,
which had collapsed and trapped him and his friends under tons of
rubble. They didn't know how deeply buried they were, so their first
instinct was to push up in an attempt to escape. Furniss and his friends
soon discovered the futility of those efforts.

His parents, meanwhile, were frantic. Kevin's father Bob was in
Las Vegas on a business trip, and he got word from his wife Susan

11

about the tornado. They had both been trying to call Kevin, with no success.

"If you knew my son, we're in constant contact," Bob said. "For him not to answer was a pretty big deal."

Bob started getting calls from friends expressing concern. They had heard about the tornado hitting Union. Was Kevin OK?

Bob didn't know.

The first hour passed with much screaming, much chaos, and much panic for Kevin and his friends. They tried desperately to get someone—anyone—to hear their cries for help.

Shortly thereafter, Jordan Thompson, one of Kevin's friends, managed to free himself from the debris and simply sat in a cave-like opening in the darkness. He began talking to Kevin and his friends, encouraging them in their distress.

"We started praying and reciting the Scripture," Furniss said. "I sang a little bit. Jordan joined in."

Part of the reason Kevin's demeanor improved was because he wasn't in pain anymore. He had gone numb. Their spirits lifted, the young men began joking around with each other. They talked about what they had done that afternoon and where they were going to eat when they got out. After the second hour had passed, Jordan got out of the collapsed building entirely.

When that happened, Kevin said things got worse—because there was no one with them to encourage them. By that time, however, Kevin could feel the emergency workers getting closer with their equipment. It didn't bring the hope that Kevin had expected.

"The sledge hammer and the chainsaw were the worst, because you could feel the sledge hammer jamming everything tighter. And you could hear the chainsaw," Furniss said. "The scariest thing was not the tornado. It wasn't being trapped and thinking I was going to suffocate. It wasn't being afraid I was going to have broken bones. The scariest thing was that the chainsaw was going to go into my back."

He no longer had feeling in his legs. He questioned whether he'd ever be able to play tennis again. He feared for the safety of his friends who were also buried just a few feet away.

Sometimes he even hoped that death would come swiftly.

"I actually told myself that if they weren't coming quick, I wanted my lungs to lock up," Furniss said.

But God had other plans for him, and the rescue workers knew what they were doing. Slowly and skillfully, they finally removed enough of the debris—in part guided by Kevin's verbal instructions—to allow Kevin to punch his hand out through the sheet rock above him into the cold night air.

"A firefighter actually grabbed it," Furniss said. "It was hope, and it was life. It really did feel like he gave me life just by touching my hand."

For Furniss, the feeling brought back memories of another time in his life when he needed to be rescued.

"It felt a lot like when I prayed to receive Christ," he recalled. "He pulled me out of a lot of sin. As deep and hopeless as I was, Christ pulled me out. In the same way, it felt that way when the firefighter grabbed my hand and pulled me out.

"When I reached my hand out and started waving it around, I was hoping for someone to touch it, or feel water on it, or something that wasn't underground," Furniss said. "And then out of nowhere the guy—I couldn't see, I didn't know who he was, but it was another life, and he squeezed my hand and told me that they were there. He actually tried to let it go, probably to help get me out, and I wouldn't let him let go.

"It felt like I was underground and had no hope and no future. I was 25 feet deep, and the moment he touched my hand it was life."

His memories grow hazy at that point. He remembers getting placed onto a stretcher, and he remembers how comfortable it felt. About this time, his mother finally got word from paramedics that Kevin was alive, breathing on his own, and en route to the hospital. She relayed the news to her husband, who was boarding a flight home.

At the hospital Kevin also remembers getting the word that all of his friends had been rescued. Though some of their injuries were serious, all of them were alive and would ultimately pull through.

"That was news I didn't ever think I'd hear," Kevin said.

In the hours ahead, while lying in his hospital bed, Kevin's thoughts turned to his friends—especially his best friend Jason Kaspar, who would spend several days in intensive care. He also began to ask a perfectly normal question: Why?

But the question was not the one typically asked by those with little faith: Why did God allow this to happen to me? Instead, Kevin's question displayed a healthy understanding of God's sovereignty and providence: Why am I still alive?

"I really didn't understand why I was alive, because I really shouldn't be," he said.

His injuries kept him in the hospital for six days, but they didn't weaken his trust in the Lord. Through it all, Furniss has found peace in clinging to the Savior who lifted him from his sin and gave him new life—spiritual life, which Furniss knows he can never lose.

The next morning at about 9 a.m., Kevin's dad finally arrived at the hospital.

"It was a very long fourteen hours," Bob said. "He looked much better than I expected. I hugged him."

Bob fought back tears as he recounted the moment.

"The times that are hard, as a dad, are when you get quiet and realize how close he was to death," he said.

Though hurting, Kevin gladly granted all kinds of interviews to the media. He spoke to FOX News' Greta Van Susteren, to the CBS Nightly News with Katie Couric, to Memphis' *Commercial Appeal* and to *The Jackson Sun*, among others. He took every opportunity to talk to the world about the Lord.

"The reason I kept doing interviews was because those other guys couldn't, and I wanted the gospel out," he said.

He was discouraged at times when producers axed the most potent statements about his faith. The CBS account was stripped of almost everything Kevin said about Jesus Christ. But, he quickly points out, there were five people on the crew in his room who heard what he had to say.

His acknowledgment of God's work did manage to make it out in other ways. In the *Commercial Appeal*, Furniss was quoted as saying, "This was the first time in my life that I've ever prayed when I was in trouble. I knew this was something I couldn't fix myself, and I had to rely on Jesus Christ to get me through it.

"It's uncomfortable and I'm hurting, but I couldn't be happier," he continued in the story. "I'm alive. We all are. This is nothing short of a miracle."

And in *The Jackson Sun*, Furniss had this to say: "I have so much trust in God's will for my life. He must have something planned for me."

Upon his discharge from the hospital six days after admission, Furniss and his family drove straight to the Union campus. Kevin wanted to see where he had been trapped. At first, when he approached the pile of rubble that had enveloped him, a policeman reprimanded him.

"Hey, you're too close. Get away from that," the man said.

But then someone explained to the officer who Kevin was, and the man's demeanor changed. He helped Kevin walk onto the top of the pile, where days before Kevin and his friends had been buried alive.

"I sat up there with my dad," Kevin said. "We cried a little bit, and we prayed."

Seeing the extent of the devastation for the first time caused Kevin to wonder at God's mercy in sparing him, and in sparing everyone else on campus.

"I don't know why no one was killed, much less myself," he said. "I don't know why hundreds of girls weren't killed."

The only thing he could think was that God had a reason for him to be alive—that God somehow would glorify Himself through the events of February 5. Kevin didn't have to wait long to see what he considers to be at least a part of God's purposes in allowing the tornado to happen. Only a few days after the tragedy, one of his close friends, Chris Lean, became a Christian.

"He realized he didn't have what we had, and he is now a believer," Kevin said. "To hear that news, it really made it all worth it."

After having some time to process it all, Kevin also had some better insight into what the calamity meant for him personally.

"It really gives me a better understanding of my salvation, the fact that I'm alive spiritually," Furniss said. "It compares greatly with why I'm alive physically now. I'm amazed by how awesome God is, how powerful and in control He is.

"God could have been doing a bunch of other stuff that night than climbing down in a hole and sitting there with us. But Christ was down there with us by His choice. I don't understand the love Christ has. All the attributes you read about Christ really came true for me that night."

Kevin Furniss thinks about his time trapped under a collapsed building every time he walks into a new room. Upon entering, he thinks to himself, "What will I do if this room collapses?"

It's an understandable reaction, given the three hours Furniss spent wondering if he'd live long enough to see another day.

But he knows these are only lingering effects from his entrapment. And in days and weeks after February 5, he found the words of the prophet Jeremiah especially meaningful: "'For I know the plans I have for you'—this is the LORD's declaration—'plans for your welfare, not for disaster, to give you a future and a hope'" (29:11).

# Elizabeth Walker

Junior, Digital media studies major from Louisville, Kentucky

*Missy was looking through the window of my room and she said that she could see the tornado. Most of us got up to check it out, then a bolt of lightning hit. All I could see was a gray purple sky with wind rushing everywhere. Then I felt the pressure in my head that pushed my back into my bookshelf. A loud train whistle sound filled the room as I was thrown to the ground.*

*I felt debris and water rushing against my face. That's all I remember for a while. Then I remember I couldn't really hear anything. I couldn't move anything. All I could do was think. I realized that I was in the hallway between my bedroom and the bathroom and our couch was on top of me. A few minutes later I was able to get up and I saw the devastation around me. The girls in the bathroom were crying and talking on their phones or texting. I looked at my phone and saw a text from my dad asking me if I was OK.*

*I thought to myself, I don't know if I am OK, so I texted him two words: "I'm alive."*

*There is no way I would be here today without the help of the Lord. Jesus Christ alone is the Savior of the world and He proves Himself faithful in all things. If you do not know Him personally, then you not only will miss out on an eternity in heaven, but also on a relationship that will change your life and shape every bit of who you are.*

# JULIE BOYER:
# A PRAYER OF DESPERATION

2001 Union University graduate, Snohomish, Washington

*"The* LORD *your God is among you, a warrior who saves. He will rejoice over you with gladness. He will bring you quietness with His love. He will delight in you with shouts of joy."*
*(Zephaniah 3:17)*

"Jesus, I need you."

That was Julie Boyer's prayer the night of February 5. She prayed it while lying in a bathtub, suffocating and crushed by 15 feet of debris from the building that had collapsed on top of her.

Like so many others at Union University, Julie escaped without serious injuries. Like so many others, she has a story to tell about how God was with her that night, and about how she was a beneficiary of the miraculous.

"I know this is something God did for His glory and His glory alone," Boyer said. "It's very evident because we had a building fall on us, and we did nothing to get ourselves out but rely on the Lord."

As a resident of a second-floor apartment in a complex just across the street from the Union campus, Julie knew with the incoming storm that she would have to find shelter in a safer place. Her downstairs neighbors weren't home, so she decided to come to Union and ride out the storm with some of the young women to whom she is a mentor—Kellie Roe, Heather Martin, and Suzanne Short.

She figured she could spend the time in their room (Jelks 11) visiting and having fun. Just in case she needed it, she brought her "tornado bag" with her, filled with pajamas, dinner, her favorite Bible, another book she was reading, a first aid kit, a flashlight, and her purse.

For some reason she can't explain, she felt the need to call her father and let him know where she was going.

"Dad, this may sound strange, but I feel like I need to tell you that I'm going to Jelks 11," she told him. "Write this down. Here are the names of the girls who live there."

Joining Julie and her friends in their downstairs room were three women who came down from upstairs. Suzanne had left the room for a while to perform her duties as a resident assistant, warning the residents under her care to take the necessary shelter.

As they were tracking the storm on TV, and only two minutes before the tornado's arrival, Suzanne burst back into the room with an authoritative warning:

"Get in the tub, NOW!"

Julie's own written account provides a chilling picture of what happened next.

> We moved instantly to the bathroom. The three upstairs girls climbed into the tub, bobsled style. They were positioned toward the end of the tub with the faucet. Kellie, Heather, and I stood by the edge of the tub debating whether or not we should close the bathroom door. If we did, we couldn't hear the TV. We thought the storm was still two or three minutes away. All of a sudden, the wind picked up and baseball sized hail or debris started hitting the outside door and windows. We immediately moved to close the bathroom door the rest of the way.

> At that moment, my ears popped. I've been extremely close to three other tornadoes in my life, and the pressure always changes making me swallow in order to pop my ears. Never, though, has the pressure changed instantly, forcing my ears to pop. I looked at Kellie and Heather and said, "Girls, pressure change. Get in the bathtub now!" Heather said later that my face was a mixture of shock and disbelief. I knew we were about to be hit hard.

Julie, Heather, and Kellie began squeezing to fit in the bathtub. As they struggled and the debris swirled, the bathroom wall itself crumbled on top of them. Before long, the ceiling collapsed as well. Finally, the outside brick wall came crashing down—three layers, all pressing down with immense force on Julie and her friends.

"It became silent instantly," Boyer said. "I read that the tornado only lasted thirty-seven seconds. It was fast, but the minutes following the storm lasted an eternity. The weight above us was still shifting as it became silent. It was at this moment that I realized I could barely breathe."

The pressure of tons of debris, her cramped quarters, and her contorted position all made breathing nearly impossible for Julie. Her first thoughts were that she would suffocate before rescuers could possibly find her. She considered that her life might be over, and she accepted it with calmness. *I have no regrets,* she thought.

In the confusing moments ahead, Julie discovered that of all her friends in the tub, she was hurt the worst. She was thankful for that realization.

"It would have been harder for me if another girl had been hurt and I wasn't able to help her because we couldn't move," Julie said. "These thoughts were not heroic or noble. I think this was my thought pattern because I am older and have lived more life. I don't know. What I do know is that God was in the midst of us in the tub that night."

While rescue workers were on their way, Julie struggled mightily just to breathe. Heather, who was on top of her, tried to move to alleviate the pressure on Julie, but it only made things worse. Julie began to pray, but then realized that by focusing on her prayer, she was forgetting to breathe.

Again, Julie's written account:

> I told God I was sorry, but I couldn't pray anymore or I wouldn't remember to take my next breath. Heather didn't know this since it was in my head, but the next thing she said was, "Julie, don't try to pray, just breathe. I'm interceding for you. Focus on breathing."
>
> It was the sweetest moment of the whole night for me. No one else knew that (the previous) Sunday night Heather called me and said she didn't know what to pray for anymore. She asked me to start interceding for her before our God. Three weeks prior, one of

her dearest friends died in an avalanche in Colorado. Heather was still grieving and struggling through Lygon's death. I prayed that night for over an hour. The next night, the one before the tornado, Heather called to say thank you. I told her it was my privilege as her sister in Christ, and I knew she would do the same for me someday. I never imagined it would be the next night during a fight for my life.

I told God I was OK with dying but that He needed to save my life for Heather. "You promise not to give us more than we can handle, Lord, but I don't think Heather can handle another death in her life. I have to live, Jesus. Heather couldn't take it." Then I focused on breathing again.

Deprived of oxygen, Julie began sliding in and out of consciousness. And the arrival of rescue workers wasn't the end of the threat. As the rescuers worked through the debris, it often caused even more pressure to build up on Julie. Heather couldn't move because it made Julie's predicament more precarious. To make matters worse, Julie's neck was positioned in such a way that if the rescue workers had slid the debris off instead of lifting it off, they would have snapped her neck.

Heather was trying to communicate that to the firefighters, who tried to calm her because they thought she was panicking. Heather finally succeeded in making eye contact with one of them.

"Can you see my face?" she asked.

"Yes," he replied.

"I am not panicking," she told him. "You have to listen to me. There is someone stuck under me and if I move, she can't breathe. Her neck is exposed, so you can't slide the debris. You have to lift it."

They followed her instructions, and after 45 minutes of entrapment, Julie could finally breathe again. Doctors later told her that two more minutes of entrapment would have killed her.

She remembers the beauty of the firefighters leaning over her. She remembers seeing that Heather's legs never made it into the tub, and that in the midst of all the debris engulfing them, the only gap was where a 2-by-4 board had kept the weight off Heather's legs.

She remembers being held by Union student Luke Burleson after the firemen pulled her from the tub.

She remembers thinking that his embrace must be similar to the arms of God: safe, secure, strong, and warm.

"I know my Jesus in a more intimate way than ever before," she said. "My God is truly mighty to save. He can move mountains, and He moved the mountain of rubble off of us that night.

"I know my days are numbered, but I will not leave this earth until Jesus says it is time. I will proclaim His glory, His grace, and His strength until then. I had peace about my death that night, and I have peace about my life right now."

# David Wickiser

Junior, Biblical languages major from Centerville, Tennessee

I started the night in McAfee commons, in the bathroom with about ten other guys. The power went out but we still had wireless Internet and were checking the radars, when all of a sudden we noticed the pressure changed. When someone mentioned it, we freaked out and heard the tornado in the background, followed by the sound of all the glass in McAfee shattering.

Soon some people walked in who were in a car, and they were torn up pretty badly. We walked out of the commons and it was surreal—seeing walls just torn off as they were and roofs missing.

When we got out of McAfee, we realized how blessed we were. We saw the trees that were split standing in the ambient light, along with the pile of cars—with a red one jutting noticeably higher. There was no clear path.

On our way a National Guardsman pulled about eight guys to try and help at Watters. When we got over there we were horrified. There were a few feet of walls and the rest just rubble. We had to dodge walls and sections of roof lying everywhere. We could hear a few of the guys that were still trapped underneath the rubble, but there wasn't enough room and too many other people for us to do anything. I have never felt so helpless. It is truly a miracle there was no one killed.

# DANNY SONG:
# A SOFA OF SHELTER

Junior, Jackson, Tennessee

*"After the earthquake there was a fire, but the LORD was
not in the fire. And after the fire there was a voice,
a soft whisper." (1 Kings 19:12)*

S ummer missions or summer camp?
That was Danny Song's dilemma as he prepared for the summer months. As he ate dinner with his girlfriend Sarah Logan on February 5, Song was talking with her about the two options. He was leaning toward doing summer missions, because he thought it would be more difficult.

"I remember telling her that I feel like I want to pick the harder thing, because I feel like that way God will move more and I'll be able to see God more," Song said. "It's not that God's going to be in it any more or any less, but it's just that I'll be able to see Him more clearly if it's something that I know is outside of my own power, and something that I'm incapable of doing myself."

Song didn't have to wait until summer to get his wish to see God at work more clearly. Less than two hours later, Song would find himself pinned under a couch and trapped beneath a fallen building. He discovered quickly just how incapable he was of rescuing himself.

After finishing dinner, Song, a resident assistant in the Watters housing complex, reported for work in the Watters commons building. He sat there watching the weather reports on TV and dismissing the predictions of tornadic activity.

*Well, I've heard that,* Song thought to himself. *I've lived in Jackson for six years. I've heard that at least three times a year.* It was a "no big deal" kind of thing.

Mario Cobo, the residence director of the Watters complex, asked Danny to turn on the tornado siren. As it blared over the intercom system, Song began getting calls from residents, asking him to turn it off. He quit answering the telephone.

*It's just going to be on because my boss told me to keep it on,* he thought.

Then Aaron Gilbert and Matt Taylor rushed into the building.

"Guys, the tornado is here!" they said. "It's right outside, so we need to take cover!"

As a typical guy, Song took that warning as an invitation to look outside and see it for himself.

"We ran outside the door to look, and we just opened the door and I remember there were six of us huddled there looking," Danny said. "It was like, 'Oh, my gosh! There it is!' We stared at it, and it was like we were just frozen there until finally there was a streak of lightning across the sky. It kind of woke us up from our daze and we were like, 'Oh, my gosh! We need to get out of here!'"

The guys scattered. Danny scrambled for the hallway where he was planning to take cover. He didn't make it.

"All the windows around me just exploded, and it wasn't like something hit it and it broke," Song said. "It was just like the windows evaporated."

Song fell to the floor and tried to cover himself. He felt a mighty wind swirling around him. As he huddled in the middle of the floor, a couch rammed against him and wedged his foot to the ground.

*Oh, my goodness,* Danny thought. *It's sucking this couch out, so it's going to suck me out.*

He thought he felt a table fall on him. Then the building caved in. All of a sudden, it was quiet. Before he had a chance to get his bearings, a piercing voice jolted Song back to coherence.

"Help!" Matt Taylor cried.

Danny tried to get up. He then discovered that what he thought was a table was actually a concrete wall that had fallen on him.

"The reason it didn't crush me was because the couch was next to me," Song said. "The couch ended up holding up that wall, and it created like a little wedge for me."

Song was on his knees in the fetal position, face down. The wedge created by the couch and the wall was just big enough for him. He tried to lift himself up, but he couldn't move. Something was also digging into his leg.

"I didn't know if it was pierced or what," Danny said. "I didn't know if I was bleeding because I couldn't reach back to feel my legs."

Danny began to hear the voices of friends—like Aaron Gilbert and Joe Ball—so he knew they were free. Taylor was closer to the surface, so they could see him. But because Danny was deeper under the debris, he wasn't visible.

"They were talking to (Matt) because he was more panicked, but I was starting to feel a little bit scared," Song said. "I hope they don't forget that I'm here, too. I wanted them to take care of Matt first, because obviously he was hurt more than I was. But at the same time, it was so hard for me not to be selfish, because my legs were losing circulation. They were burning—that burning, tingling sensation all throughout."

The rescue workers arrived quickly and began working to free Taylor. Lee Benson, a Union University art professor, was also on the scene talking to Matt as the firemen worked to free him. Danny recognized Benson's voice, as Benson had been Song's Sunday school teacher in high school.

"Mr. Lee! Mr. Lee! Mr. Lee!" Danny called.

Benson heard Song calling him, but he didn't know where the voice was coming from.

"I shined my flashlight back under the slab, and all I could see were a couple of eyes back there," Benson said.

"Who is that?" Benson asked.

"This is Danny!" Song yelled back.

Benson stayed with Danny, encouraging him and praying for him.

"It was really good to hear his voice, and just hear people trying to help," Song said.

Song's cell phone also provided additional comfort. Although it was in his pocket, he couldn't reach it because he was in an awkward position. But it was ringing constantly, and he could hear the text messages coming in.

When he was first trapped, the questions started coming to him. What about the rest of the campus? How bad is it? Is Sarah OK? Are my roommates OK?

"Every time my phone rang, I remember thinking, *OK, maybe that's one of them calling me and telling me they're OK and looking for me,* he said.

After about an hour, the firemen freed Matt. Song looked up and saw him as Taylor yelled, "Danny, I'm out, brother!"

"Pray for me!" Song called back.

With Taylor rescued, the firemen could turn their attention to Danny. During the process Benson noticed that a fireman had laid a towel over Danny's face.

"Is he dead?" Benson asked.

"We're doing the best we can," the fireman replied.

"I want to know if he's dead," Benson insisted. "I'm not leaving here until I know if he's alive or dead."

"We think he's alive," the fireman said.

Benson thinks Song may have gone to sleep.

"Either he passed out or he went to sleep," Benson said. "I actually thought he had passed away."

One fireman, Matt Gay, had slipped into the pocket with Danny and stood above him cutting debris with a chainsaw. He had removed everything he could, but a bundle of 2-by-4 boards across Danny's back kept him pinned down and prevented him from sliding out. Gay didn't want to cut that bundle, because he thought it might be holding up the concrete slab above Song. Removing that support would have meant certain death for both him and Song.

"I had cut everything else except for that, and that was the strongest thing that was there," Gay said. "He wasn't going to come out, and there was nothing else we could do."

Gay discussed the situation with his captain. By now Danny was conscious again, but he was starting to become unresponsive.

"I didn't know if he was injured really badly, but I knew in the position he was in he definitely didn't have any circulation," Gay said.

Gay cut the top of the boards to see if they would pinch the blade. That would be a sign indicating a high amount of pressure on those boards. And sure enough, they pinched the blade immediately. He stepped back, looked at the boards, and continued to debate with himself.

"I finally just said, 'The heck with it. We're going to do it,'" Gay said.

Danny remembers Gay explaining the situation to him—that cutting the boards was a gamble that could cost them their lives.

"Well, OK," Danny thought. "I guess if he cuts this and it falls, it's going to kill both of us, not just me. I trusted him. At that point, I was just like, 'Cut the board, guys. Just get it off.'"

Gay fired up the chainsaw and sliced away. The debris pile creaked and popped. The boards moved slightly, but not enough to bring everything down on top of them. The concrete slab stayed put, and Danny was free.

"I won on that gamble," Gay said, "but I wouldn't want to make that gamble many times."

Though he went to the hospital for treatment, Song was released by 11 p.m. that night. He had some cuts and lost some feeling in his left leg for a couple of weeks, but that was it. In fact, for Song, the spiritual battle was harder than the physical one.

"Some people, I guess, could say that at those times God really comes and gives them peace and stuff," Danny said. "But, for me, I was almost resentful of God and saying, 'God didn't help me that night.' That's what I was thinking for a while. I was alive, but firemen got me out and, you know, where was God?"

Song struggled with those kinds of questions. A couch saved his life, but many might point to that simply as luck. He wanted God to have worked in a way that nobody could doubt God's activity.

He prayed for an answer. He found it in 1 Kings 19, when God appeared to Elijah—not in the mighty wind, not in the earthquake, but in the silence.

"It was a soft whisper," Song said. "It was like you can barely hear it, but He's there and He doesn't have to reveal Himself in the wind, or the fire, or the earthquake, because He is there in the silence, and He's there no matter what. Sometimes we may have to look for Him, but He just proved that night that He was there."

Danny realized that God was there when the couch kept the wall from crushing him. He was there when the firefighters spent hours in training so they would know what to do in times of crisis. He was there when Gay cut that bundle of boards, and the wall didn't move.

And the more he talked to his friends who survived that night, the more Song realized just how evident God's hand was.

"He chose to reveal His glory through everybody He saved at Union that day," Danny said. "It's not about us. It's not about Union and especially not about me. It's just about God showing Himself to us, and in His mercy and providence, He saw fit that He would reveal His glory that night by saving us."

# Meredyth Moyers

Junior, Marketing major from Sikeston, Missouri

*As evening approached, I knew the weather was going to get bad. I used to watch the Weather Channel for fun, so I knew that a 30-degree temperature drop in the forecast was a good indicator of severe weather. I honestly expected a tornado, but the question was when and where.*

*The sky was blood red, and the funnel was forming over near Jennings Hall and the intramural field. It was so close. The lightning was so bright. The second we saw it, we tried to run back to the bathroom. It was so loud and sounded like a freight train, like they say. We didn't make it in time. In a split second, it was dead quiet, then BOOM! It hit. All of our ears were popping and everyone was screaming. I felt glass and debris rushing by my head. Then, I saw green and blue lights everywhere, which we later found out was the lightning from inside the funnel. We were INSIDE it!*

*We all thought for sure we were going to die. One of my shoes flew off, but I amazingly had my phone. The ceiling was falling, and I looked up to see sky and the room above us gone. We thought maybe the tornado was still here since the room above us was caving in on us.*

*It was dead silent. I'm told you could hear only the eerie sound of everyone's cell phone rings all around the campus and that was it. No screaming; no yelling; just ringing. The phone calls and texts from fellow students, alums, family members, and high school friends poured in. I finally cried and had it all out. We made sure everyone of our friends was OK. We went back up to campus later and asked security how everyone was. Miraculously everyone who was buried made it out and no one died.*

# CHRIS LEAN:
# A STORY OF CONVERSION

Senior, Vancouver, British Columbia

*"For the Son of Man has come to seek and to save the lost."*
*(Luke 19:10)*

Chris Lean wasn't in harm's way when the tornado hit Union University. He wasn't trapped by a fallen building, nor was he afraid for his life.

In fact, he wasn't even on campus that night.

But through the tornado, God saved Lean, a senior from Vancouver, British Columbia, even more than those who found themselves trapped under the rubble. For Lean's friends in that predicament, their salvation was physical.

Lean's salvation, meanwhile, was spiritual.

"It's an amazing testimony about what the Lord can do through what would seem like tragic events," said Scott Marksberry, the assistant coach for Union's men's soccer team, about Chris's story.

His story of salvation began in 1999, when he started coming to Union for soccer camps. His older brother Jeff played soccer at Union from 1999–2002, and Chris often visited him. He met Marksberry, a teammate of Jeff's, during this time.

"We started to build a relationship back then," Marksberry said. "Most of it was college guys messing with a high school kid."

Chris knew he'd ultimately follow his brother to the Jackson, Tennessee, university.

"I didn't really even look elsewhere," he said.

Lean grew up in a good home—a moral home—but one where God certainly was not emphasized.

"When I first came to Union, I believed that there was a God," Lean said. "I didn't know anything about Him. I had no clue. I couldn't have told you anything about the Bible. I never looked at it, when I first came here."

Needless to say, when he arrived on campus in 2002, Chris experienced something of a culture shock. The campus was full of Christians who talked openly about their faith. The university even required classes like Old Testament Survey and New Testament Survey.

Chris sat through those classes and listened to stories from the Bible—stories he had never heard before. He shook his head in disbelief. A great fish swallowing Jonah? A chariot of fire carrying Elijah to heaven? Jesus feeding five thousand people with five loaves of bread and two fish?

Come on.

"I just didn't believe them," Lean said. "I would read them and say, 'This is impossible. This doesn't make sense to me at all.'"

After his freshman year, Lean went home for a year before returning to Union in 2004. That year he started dating a girl and went to church with her for about a year.

"I tried," he said. "It was always a fight. It would never hit home for me."

He heard about his soccer teammates becoming Christians and was skeptical. He thought they were doing it for their girlfriends. Chris would have none of it.

"I resisted it pretty good the first couple of years here," he said.

Lean began to notice a shift in his thinking about spiritual matters when Marksberry returned as the soccer team's assistant coach.

He also credits the new head coach, Clovis Simas, as contributing to that shift.

"They really brought a spiritual side to the team that hadn't been there before," Chris said. "I still fought it, but there was more there. I kind of got more open to it."

One of Chris' big obstacles to becoming a Christian was what he saw from a few friends who claimed to be Christians, and yet their lives didn't match up with what they professed.

"That really bothered him," Marksberry said. "He was always expressing that as his main concern: 'I don't see how you can be a Christian and do the same things that I'm doing.'"

But Marksberry consistently countered that pattern of thinking.

"It's not about your relationship with that guy, who says he's a Christian," Marksberry told him. "It's about your relationship with Jesus."

Over the past year or so Lean began thinking even more about his spiritual condition. Several "coincidences"—what he called them at the time—gave him pause.

For example, during the 2006 season Lean was the only varsity-level goalkeeper on the team. During a light warm-up the day before Union's first conference game, his groin muscle popped. He fell to the ground in pain, devastated and heartbroken because he knew he'd most likely miss several games.

"Coach Clovis and Scott pulled me into their office that night and prayed over me and asked God somehow to heal me," Chris recalled. "When they prayed over me in the office, it brought me to tears."

He hardly slept that night because he was in too much pain. The next morning, although he couldn't put any weight on his right leg, he decided he was going to try to play—with a heavily-taped leg and a healthy dose of ibuprofen coursing through his veins.

Chris couldn't warm up. He couldn't dive. And Union's opponent, Martin Methodist, was a tough team. Lean knew it wasn't going to be a good day.

But somehow, some way, Union won the game 3 to 1. Martin Methodist's only goal came on a penalty kick. Other than that, they didn't get a single shot off the entire game.

Over the next four games, with Lean hobbling in the goal, Union gave up only seven total shots. Until that point, the team had typically allowed 8 to 15 shots per game.

Coincidence? Maybe to some. But to Lean, it was an early sign that God was watching out for him.

Fast forward to February 5. The day had a familiar feel to Chris, who was on campus in 2002 when another tornado hit the Union campus. In comparison to 2008, the 2002 tornado was a pipsqueak.

"All the signs were the same for me," he said. "I had the feeling it was going to be a rough night."

He had no idea how right he was.

Lean was visiting some friends off campus when the tornado struck. He heard reports on the radio that Union had been hit.

"I still thought, 2002," Chris said. "Not a huge thing."

He tried calling his friend David Wilson. No answer.

So he tried another friend, Kevin Bradley. No answer.

He began to get worried as he heard more and more reports about the situation at Union. Around 9 p.m. he heard that students were trapped. An hour later he found out that his friends were the victims.

"When I found out it was David, it was the first, true, honest time I'd ever prayed," Lean said. "I prayed for God to take care of him."

He tried to return to campus, but he couldn't get access. Another storm was moving in, so he went back to his friends' home. Later that night, when David Wilson was rescued and taken to the hospital, Chris rushed to the trauma unit to be by his friend's side.

Throughout the night Chris felt helpless, a feeling he despised. He couldn't get to campus to help his friends in their time of need. With several of them lying in the hospital, he couldn't do anything to make them better.

He quickly encountered some other people who felt helpless— David Wilson's family. David had spent five hours trapped in a collapsed building. Now he was in a hospital bed in intensive care.

"There was a lot of praying, obviously," Lean said. "I was seeing his parents and his family leaving it all up to God. Everything that was happening, they just put it in His hands. I was seeing first hand how much people did believe in Him and trust Him."

He had only met David's parents once or twice before. But in the days after the tornado, he became a part of their family. He was with them constantly at the hospital. He saw their faith in action.

A few days after the tornado, someone found David's Bible in the dorm wreckage and brought it to the hospital. Chris asked if he could borrow it. It was the first time he had ever opened up a Bible and started reading it.

"I don't know why," he said. "I just did it. That night I read some passages that (David) had highlighted."

The following Sunday Chris decided to attend a worship service at Englewood Baptist Church. He went by himself—another first.

"From start to finish, I was in tears," Lean said. "I just couldn't control it. That was actually the very first time where I felt like God was talking to me. That was huge for me. I'd never felt that."

Later that week he went back to the Union campus with some of David's family members to pick up David's stuff. For the first time since the tornado, Chris saw the men's commons building—where his friends had been trapped for hours—lying in a jumbled mess.

"I looked at the rubble, and I started to get upset," Lean said. "There's no way anybody should be alive. I couldn't put my head around it."

He began to think back to those Old Testament and New Testament survey classes—the ones where he heard about the miracles that he didn't believe.

The thought hit him: This was no less of a miracle than those stories.

"For no one to be dead after that is a miracle," Lean said. "That's what made me a believer."

That night he was with some friends at their apartment. Soccer was the typical topic of discussion for the group of guys. But this night, at about 1 a.m., the conversation turned to religion and spiritual matters.

Throughout the discussion the lights went on for Lean. The rubble pile earlier in the day had started it, and the conversation that night had confirmed it. He understood clearly what Marksberry and others had been telling him—that Jesus Christ was his only hope for salvation.

And—like so many other firsts in Chris' life—for the first time, he believed.

At 5:30 a.m. he sent Marksberry a text message: "We need to talk."

Marksberry was asleep when that message came. When he awoke later in the morning, he read that message and listened to a voice mail message from Chris saying that he wanted to become a Christian.

"I was extremely excited," Marksberry said. "I went running in to my wife, who was still asleep: 'You'll never believe this. Chris Lean just called and says that he's really serious about learning more about Jesus.'"

That morning Lean went to the hospital to see David, and to tell him the news: "I've decided to accept Christ in my life."

David's response?

"I would go through this all again, just to hear that," he said.

Lean met Marksberry in the hall outside David's room, where they sat and talked for nearly three hours. He told Marksberry his story about the day before, and that he was trusting in Christ. But he still had some trouble with a few things.

"You've known Jesus in your life personally for five hours," Marksberry replied. "You're definitely not going to have answers to all the questions right now. Just be patient. Let's start to work through some Scripture and some of these specific issues that you know you want to deal with."

As they talked, Marksberry emphasized to Lean the importance of learning more about Jesus, of making Him bigger in his life. When that happens, Scott said, all the little issues are going to start sorting themselves out.

In the weeks following Chris' conversion, Marksberry has definitely seen a difference.

"There's a change relationally with him, in the way he relates to everybody around here," Marksberry said. "He's always been a very outgoing guy, a talkative, expressive guy. But now his conversations are a bit more intentional. When he talks to somebody, he's not afraid to be open about this change in his life."

For Marksberry, Chris' story of salvation was nine years in the making.

"The fact that it happened through a tornado is another testament to the fact that it's never about what we say to a guy," Marksberry said. "And I'm glad that God reminds us about those kinds of things—that it's not going to be about the words that I put into Chris' ear, but it's going to be about what God does in his life."

# Katie Mitchell

Sophomore, Christian studies major from Little Rock, Arkansas

*One girl warned us that we would know it was coming when the plumbing made a sucking sound. Soon enough the sucking sound came and we all dove on the floor of the bathroom. The walls and ceiling were ripped off of that bathroom and we saw the tornado above us.*

*We proceeded to the dorm next door only to be told there was a gas leak and we needed to get to the McAfee commons. After we finally got people piled in the stairwell and got settled for maybe 10 minutes, we were being yelled at to move again. There seemed to be a gas leak in McAfee.*

*The next place of destination was White Hall, and, if you know anything about the campus, you know that the walk from McAfee to White Hall is extremely long. While walking I saw cars flipping and flying, fallen power lines, and dorms that were no longer recognizable.*

*It is a miracle that no one died. We serve a big and amazing God.*

# CHERYL PROPST:
# A BOARD OF PROTECTION

Sophomore, Arusha, Tanzania

*"I will not die, but I will live and proclaim what the*
Lord *has done." (Psalm 118:17)*

A crazy thought entered Cheryl Propst's mind as she rode in the ambulance to the hospital.

Every turn and every jostle caused her excruciating pain—especially the speed bumps as they approached the emergency room.

*Why do they have speed bumps going into the ER?* Cheryl thought to herself. *Don't you want to get there faster?*

While the logic of that is hard to deny, Cheryl's purpose in analyzing the matter wasn't logic. It was to keep her mind off the immense pain shooting through her body.

Cheryl, a sophomore at Union from Tanzania, where her parents served as missionaries, was admittedly ignorant about tornadoes prior to the one that hit the Union campus February 5. Africa is not known for its twisters.

So when she went running in the late afternoon and noticed the sky getting dark, she was not worried. Even when the tornado sirens sounded, it wasn't a huge deal. Cheryl was hanging out in her room with her roommate Katy and a couple of other girls, Ashley Bruski and Raquel Mack.

"I was kind of curious to see what was going on," Propst said. "I was looking out and talking to people across the way."

But her curiosity turned to concern as she began to hear the wind coming.

43

"It was like a jet engine coming right at you," she said. "When I first heard it, it didn't click in my brain that it was actually a tornado coming."

That changed when she heard one of the girls in her room cry out, "We've got to go to the bathroom!" That's when it hit Cheryl that this was real.

Cheryl was the first one into the bathroom, and she sat down in the bathtub as she had been instructed. She didn't have to wait long to see the power of the tornado that had made her so curious only moments before.

"As soon as I got in and sat down, everything started ripping apart and crashing," Cheryl said. "I could feel my hair sticking up. It was weird."

The bathroom door slammed. Then Cheryl got hit on the left side of her back, by what she doesn't know. Maybe it was a cinder block. But whatever it was, it packed a mighty wallop.

"There's no way to describe the pain," she said. "It was immediate."

All of a sudden she was soaking wet. Dirt was everywhere, and she was covered in mud. Grimacing from the pain, she looked up to see that all the walls of the bathroom were gone.

Cheryl reached over next to her in the bathtub, but nobody was there. So she lay down and stayed there until the storm had passed. When it did, she began to think about the girls who should have been in the tub beside her.

*Where are they?* Propst asked herself. *Are they going to be lying here dead beside me? Am I the only one alive after this?*

She heard Katy walking around outside, praying, "Jesus, please help us. Jesus, please help us."

*Oh yeah,* Cheryl thought. *I should be praying. I didn't even think about that.*

She didn't have time to. She heard the cries of Ashley and Raquel only a few feet away from her.

"Help! Get us out! Get us out!"

Cheryl knew they were trapped. She helped pull the boards off one girl, then she and Katy worked together to free the other one.

The whole time, Cheryl is thinking, *My back hurts so bad.*

The girls walked over to a grassy area to regroup and decide where they needed to go next.

"That's when I realized that I wasn't going anywhere," Propst said. "That's when it hit me how bad it actually hurt. As I was trying to walk, my back was popping and shifting. I could feel the bones moving."

She was also struggling to breathe, so she lay down on the grass as Katy and Ashley went to find help. Raquel, who stayed with her, soon saw fire truck lights a few yards away.

"We've got to walk over there," she told Cheryl.

"OK, if you say so," Cheryl replied.

As she walked, Propst noticed cars, glass, boards, and pieces of metal sticking out everywhere. The cars, especially, were twisted up and tossed all over the place.

*Why am I alive?* she thought. *Because if it can do that to a car, then it can do that to me.*

Shuffling barefoot through the parking lot, Cheryl collapsed halfway across. She simply could go no farther. Help came to her in the form of a fireman, who called paramedics to Cheryl's aid. They put a neck brace on her and began treating her.

As they were waiting on an ambulance, Cheryl heard one of the paramedics talking on the phone. Though he was trying to be quiet, she heard him nonetheless.

"I'm beside this girl, and she's going to be the first one to go when an ambulance comes," he said. "She's in really tough shape."

"That freaked me out," Cheryl said. "That was really scary."

The paramedics eventually loaded her in the ambulance—along with another Union student, Heather Martin—and took her to the hospital. Cheryl didn't know the nature of the problem. She just knew that her back hurt terribly. As a nurse was cutting off her clothes, she spied a large bruise on Cheryl's back.

"Whoa," the nurse said. "Has the doctor seen this?"

The doctor wanted to give her morphine for the pain, but Cheryl was reluctant. She thought it was going to knock her out, and she was scared of what might be done to her while she was out. So she declined.

Heather was in the room at the time and heard the exchange.

"Cheryl, are you crazy?" Heather piped up. "Take the morphine!"

After examinations, scans, and X-rays, doctors diagnosed Cheryl with three broken ribs—two of them broken in two places—a bruised lung and a bruised spleen. She remembers well a telephone conversation she overheard between a nurse and her sister Julie on her first night in the hospital. Perhaps the nurse thought Cheryl was asleep.

"Cheryl's OK. She's stable," the nurse reported to Julie. "But we haven't told her about the deaths in her building yet."

Jackson firemen, upon arriving on the scene at Union, had called the hospital and told them to expect one hundred deaths. Cheryl didn't find out until the next morning that despite the dire prediction, every Union student had survived.

During her painful nine days in the hospital—during which time she also had a chest tube inserted—Cheryl pondered her status as one of those survivors.

"I remember thinking, when I was sitting in the bathtub, that I could die," Cheryl said through tears. "And I wasn't scared—because I knew I was going to see Jesus, and that's the greatest thing ever. There's nothing I look forward to in life more than seeing Jesus."

Her roommates Rachel Daniel and Laura Coggin recalled visiting with Cheryl in the hospital.

"She was awake and everything when we were there," Rachel said. "She was so sweet, such an amazing godly girl with such a sweet spirit. Holding her hand and talking to her, it was so amazing just to see her alive."

Upon her release, Cheryl went to see her old dorm room—just a day before it was demolished. She got a good look the night of the tornado, and it was just as she remembered it.

"What do you say?" she asked. "You could just stand there and look. I was amazed that no one was dead."

Her father pointed out a 2-by-4 that was holding up a block wall leaning precariously toward the tub. Without that board, the wall likely would have fallen on Cheryl.

"Only God," she said.

Days later, as her recovery continued, and as she considered God's care for her, she pointed to her spine. Then she pointed to the closest rib that was broken.

"Two inches," she said. "Two inches, and I could be paralyzed."

Those are not mere coincidences for Cheryl, but a vivid picture of how God spared her life.

"God saved my life for a reason, and now it's my responsibility to tell what He has done, to show His glory to others," she said. "Yeah, it's hard remembering all this, and it's not fun. But it's like God said, 'I've not let you live for you to be silent.' That's not why people suffer. It's so we can tell others of His greatness."

# Ben Peacock

Sophomore, Marketing major from Memphis, Tennessee

*I was studying in my room upstairs when Mike Evans, my roommate and resident assistant, said we needed to head downstairs. I kind of chuckled and grabbed my computer and some things to eat and study.*

*Every tornado warning I had ever been through was seemingly a joke. Why should this one be any different? I asked myself.*

*I went downstairs, where a bunch of us guys just watched ESPN, ate, and studied. Then we went to the bathroom, heard the noise, and laughed because nothing seemed to happen. When we looked outside, we saw a gutter or two and some roofing tiles—no big deal to us. I went upstairs to my room to check on things. All of my stuff was fine.*

*Then the command to go to White Hall commenced and we all started going that way. Then we saw Dodd, ripped apart, and cars lying all over the field behind McAfee. This is huge. No more laughing, I thought.*

*We proceeded to walk between Hurt and McAfee, noticing every cars' windows blown out, but I didn't see anything at Hurt because it was too dark. The next day was quite a shock as I saw the most destruction I have ever seen. I went on two disaster relief trips during hurricanes Rita and Katrina, but none of the damage compared to this tornado.*

*When times are good, be happy, when times are bad, consider that the Lord has made both, according to Ecclesiastes 7:14.*

*Praise His name that no one died. We have much to be thankful for even in loss, how much more shall we be thankful in the plenty that we have always had?*

*The greatest thing that has happened in all of this is that the Lord Almighty is being glorified by many, and His name is being recognized by the media and shared with the masses.*

# DAVID WILSON:
# A TESTIMONY OF GRACE

Freshman, Chattanooga, Tennessee

*"Take delight in the LORD, and He will give you
your heart's desires." (Psalm 37:4)*

David Wilson can't complain too much about the tornado that
trapped him for five hours, sent him to the hospital for weeks,
and nearly cost him his legs.

The way he sees it, God was only answering his prayers.

"Ever since I was little, I've always been the good kid," Wilson
said. "I never did drugs. I never drank. I never did any of that stuff.
I never did anything wrong. So ever since I was fourteen or fifteen,
I prayed God would give me some situation that He would get me out
of that would give me a way to share my faith.

"I didn't pray that I would be in a tornado and that my legs would
not work anymore," he continued. "But I always hoped that something would happen where I could say, 'This is how God has really
saved me, and this is what Christianity really means.'"

On the night of February 5, David was supposed to have soccer
practice at a local church. When he arrived with his teammates, his
coach told them that practice was canceled, and that they should go
back to campus and find a safe place to take shelter.

"I remember driving back, and it was real windy on the road,"
Wilson recalled. "My car was shaking a little bit."

He and his friends decided that the Watters commons building
was as safe a place as any, so they passed the time playing ping pong,
waiting for the tornado to hit.

David moved to the women's bathroom in the men's commons for safety upon the request of residence director Mario Cobo. Four other guys took cover in the men's bathroom. While waiting, Wilson, Kevin Bradley, and Paul Turner decided to write a "bucket list" of things they wanted to do before they died.

Kevin Bradley, the scribe of the group, got this far: "Kevin Bradley, David Wilson, and Paul Turner on February 5 composed this bucket list . . ."

Paul had left the bathroom for a second, and David remembers what he saw upon Turner's return.

"Paul walked in the bathroom door," Wilson said. "I saw the lights flicker. And as Paul opened the door, I saw the wall behind him start to crack—the exterior wall."

Wilson jumped off the counter top and covered up on the floor as the tornado blasted them.

"We didn't actually get very far on that list," he said. "I got in the elementary tornado position, the whole hands behind your head kind of thing. I forgot about the part where you get up against a stable wall. That was kind of a key component that I forgot."

The force of the wind blew David forward onto his face and pinned his knees into his chest. The building collapsed on top of him. David couldn't move.

He and his friends quickly took stock of everyone.

"Everybody was responsive, and everybody said they were all right," Wilson said. "Nobody said they were in serious pain at the beginning. Nobody really thought they were that bad at first."

They had only been trapped for a few minutes when David remembers his friend Paul praying.

"Thank you, God, that we made it this far," Paul said. "Thank you that a board didn't hit us in the head and knock us out."

A few minutes later, Wilson felt a knee pressing against him, high up on his body.

*There's no way that's mine,* he thought.

So he thumped it.

"Paul, is this your foot?" he asked.

"No," Paul replied.

"Kevin, is that your knee?" David then asked.

"No," Kevin said.

Wilson realized that he was feeling his own knee after all.

"I was touching it, but I couldn't feel it at all," he said. "I pulled hairs out and couldn't feel anything."

By this time, David's friend Jordan, who was in the men's bathroom, made contact with the firemen and told them the names of all those who were trapped.

"He told them that we were all OK at the time, but that we really needed to get out as soon as possible," Wilson recalled.

Those who could speak were praying and singing. Kevin Furniss' voice sang out:

> How deep the Father's love for us
> How vast beyond all measure
> That He should give His only Son
> To make a wretch His treasure
>
> How great the pain of searing loss,
> The Father turns His face away
> As wounds which mar the chosen One,
> Bring many sons to glory.

The songs and prayers encouraged Wilson, who couldn't speak much because his knees were compressing his lungs. He was losing air every minute.

David was wearing a jacket, and when he jumped down onto the floor, the hood had come up on his head. The hood kept a lot of heat inside him.

Kevin Bradley, meanwhile, kept patting David on the head.

"Hang in there, Wilson," he said

"He knew I was in trouble," David said. "He knew I wasn't doing well at all."

Wilson asked Bradley if he could get the hood off his head, because he was sweating profusely. Bradley was able to remove it.

"I remember feeling a coolness come across my body," Wilson said. "It felt like a cool breeze. It felt so amazing."

The mangled debris pressing down on him prevented him from moving much at all. If he would try to move his arm, someone would yell—because it caused a shift in the debris that would hurt them.

Then the vomiting began.

Jason Kaspar was the first victim. Wilson remembers the guys telling the firemen that Kaspar was throwing up, and asking what they should do.

"As if we could have done anything," David said with a laugh. "I don't know why we asked that question."

A fireman asked how Jason was positioned—face up or face down?

"He's face down," someone replied.

"OK, he'll be fine," the fireman said. "Don't worry about it."

That report comforted David.

"That was good news, because I was face down, and I felt like I was about to throw up everything inside me," he said. "And I did."

Kevin Bradley then saw a flashlight.

"I see your light!" he yelled to the firemen. "I see your light!"

That allowed the firemen to pinpoint where the guys were located.

"How far away was that light?" David asked Kevin. "Shoot straight with me."

Bradley thought it was about 6 feet away.

"At that point, I knew we were going to get out," Wilson said. "I knew it was going to happen."

The firemen told the guys that there was a block wall on top of them that needed to be moved, and it would take a little time.

"I remember Paul Turner screaming, 'Just do it! Just get it off of us!'" David said. "It was so funny. I was like, Paul, dude, shut up. They're trying to get the wall off."

After removing the wall, the firemen began cutting with chainsaws. Kevin Bradley could smell the gas fumes from the saws and knew they were close.

David began to feel a cool breeze as the firemen closed in. Finally they made contact with David, nearly five hours after the tornado. Only he and Jason Kaspar were left, as the other five guys had been rescued. But his waist was lodged underneath the wall.

"So they put airbags in there and inflated the wall up off me," Wilson said. "I remember going up on my elbows and just breathing, taking in as much air as I could, the deepest breaths I've ever imagined."

By then Wilson had thrown up four or five times.

"They handed me a bottle of water, and I just kind of poured it all over my face," he said. "I drank some of it, but I knew if I drank too much I'd just throw up again."

He still wasn't entirely free when he heard the fireman's radio go off.

"Another storm is coming through," the voice said. "Leave the last two. Cover them with a tarp. We'll come back and get them later."

*You've got to be kidding me,* David thought. *You're not going to leave me here.*

Indeed, the firemen had no intentions of doing that.

"There's no way we're leaving these boys in here," the fireman radioed back. "We're getting them out of here."

David found his cell phone lying next to him and opened it: seventeen missed calls, thirteen new text messages. He called his dad, who was en route to Jackson from Chattanooga: "They're pulling me out of the hole. I'll see you at the hospital."

But although David was out of the hole, he wasn't out of the woods. When the firemen raised him up, his legs stayed up and didn't drop. They took him to an ambulance, where an IV was placed in each arm and a needle in his right side—because the paramedics thought his right lung had collapsed.

"The most excruciating pain I think I've ever experienced in my life was when they pulled my legs down," Wilson said. "My legs were up, and they pulled them down onto the stretcher and strapped them down. I just remember my hip flexors shooting with pain. The muscle had been so tight for five hours, and then they stretched it out."

His legs were in danger. Normally weighing in at 160 pounds, David's weight at the hospital ballooned to 220 pounds because his legs were so swollen.

The next morning, he awoke with his hands tied down and a ventilator in his mouth. By then his parents had arrived. He scribbled them a note: "Did they find all the boys?"

"My mom told me yes," David said. "And then they said I started crying after that because I was so happy that everybody got found."

A day later came the fasciotomies on his legs—four cuts in each leg to relieve the swelling—as doctors fought to save his legs from amputation. They succeeded. Though the rehabilitation is a lengthy process for Wilson—one that will take several weeks of recovery—he plans to play soccer again.

And he plans to tell his story to anyone who will listen.

"Now that I've got that story, it's going to help me a lot in sharing my faith with others," David said. "If (God) wouldn't have been there, I wouldn't be here. There's no way. There was 21 feet of stuff on top of me. What are the odds that none of it's going to hurt me?

"He definitely protected me," Wilson continued. "He protected all of us."

# Luke Tinius

Sophomore, Engineering major from Franklin, Tennessee

*My wife and I were in the Watters commons when it hit. We had been sitting in our living room eating pancakes before the sirens first went off, but when we heard them blasting, we decided that the commons would be a safe place for us to go. Little did we know that we would have been safer in our upstairs dorm than we were in the commons.*

*We were just hanging out with Mario, his wife and kids, Matt Taylor, and Aaron Gilbert. A few of us had been standing at the door next to the circle when the tornado first started to form. When I saw the tornado starting to form and the wind started picking up, we all started yelling and ran towards the small hallway next to the residence director's office.*

*We jumped into the hallway and not five seconds later the power went out, the pressure dropped, the glass shattered and began flying everywhere. I was blocking the glass from hitting my wife, Mario's wife, and his two kids. I was just praying that God would protect us, and He did.*

*The next thing I know, I hear the building fall. The loud crash was deafening, and then I felt rubble land on my back. The only thing keeping it from landing on my wife, Mario's wife, and his kids was God, who I firmly believe was between the rubble and me—because even with all the adrenaline, there is no way all that weight landed on me and I only sustained the injuries I did, which is a scratch on my hand, and a sore back and shoulders. I can't hold up that much weight with the body that God has given me. God protected us, saved us, delivered us. And the whole night long my heart sang songs of praise for the blessings He gave to us.*

# CANDACE CROSS/ ERIC SMITH: A RING OF DEVOTION

Senior, Lebanon, Tennessee/Senior, Dyersburg, Tennessee

*"Because of the LORD's faithful love we do not perish,*
*for His mercies never end. They are new every morning;*
*great is Your faithfulness!" (Lamentations 3:22–23)*

In his chest of drawers, Eric Smith had placed a wedding band for safekeeping. The ring had belonged to his great-grandmother. In a few weeks, he would place it on the finger of his fiancée, Candace Cross.

But in the mayhem following the tornado, Eric had forgotten to grab it.

Now the room above him was gone, blown away by the fierce winds. Eric's room was an absolute mess. Other possessions of his had been sucked out the window.

The day after the tornado, Candace approached a fireman with a request.

"Would you mind seeing if there's an open top drawer in that room?" she asked. "There's a ring box in there I really need."

"No, you can't do that," the fireman told her.

"I don't really want to do that," she replied. "I was hoping you could go in there for me."

He thought for a second, and then agreed. He returned carrying a drawer.

57

"I can't promise you anything's in here, because it was wide open," he said.

Anxiously Candace rummaged through the drawer.

"Lo and behold, the ring was still there," she said.

For Eric and Candace, the discovery was yet another example of God's kindness to them through the night of February 5, when for a brief period they didn't know if the other had survived.

Their relationship began during their sophomore years at Union. One Wednesday Eric was eating lunch by himself, while Candace was eating lunch with her friend Emily, who was also a friend of Eric's. Emily invited Eric to join them.

"When I sat down at that table, I just looked up and thought (Candace) was the most beautiful girl I had ever seen," Eric said. "I immediately saw that she was also very sweet, wholesome, and kind."

That night at church, Eric again talked to Candace a little bit.

"From there I made it my goal to be around her as much as I could and try to get to know her," he said.

A few weeks later Eric asked Candace out on a date.

"I thought she was resisting it, but she did say yes," he said. "I thought she was wonderful, and I wanted to marry her—as much as one can after knowing someone for a month. I had a lot of work to do."

Candace, meanwhile, was oblivious to Eric's intentions: "I was clueless until right before the call," she said.

She had decided that she was content being single. In fact, she had just told her mom to stop asking her about guys. She had reached the point where she was happy to wait for God to bring the right man into her life.

Two days later Eric called. He was obviously enamored. How long until she started to share his feelings?

"It was a good little while," Candace said. "I was really guarded."

Gradually, however, Candace did grow to love Eric the same way that he loved her. In July 2007 he asked her to marry him. She said yes.

But on the night of February 5, suddenly those wedding plans were in jeopardy. Eric and Candace had eaten dinner together and then returned to their respective rooms about thirty minutes before the tornado.

Eric was watching the Super Tuesday election returns in his room when the tornado sirens sounded. He went down to the Watters commons to say hello to his sister, Rebecca Cobo, the wife of Watters residence director Mario Cobo, and her two kids.

He went back to his room and was about to call Candace.

"All of a sudden the pressure built up in the room, real heavy," he said. "I never experienced that before. I turned around to look into the living room, and I saw the guys with their eyes real wide."

For Eric, the rest of the night was like watching a movie.

"The power went off, and then glass shattered everywhere," Eric said. "Glass is flying and the debris is coming in and hitting me in the face."

Eric and eight other guys rushed to the bathroom for shelter. As the tornado swirled, the ceiling started coming down. The pipes had burst, and water was running all over them. Then the storm stopped.

"We stepped outside, and there was just rubble everywhere," Eric said. "It really was like watching a movie. It was very surreal. I looked outside and saw the commons completely flattened, and I knew where my family was. That was a really sickening feeling, because I thought that surely they must be dead.

"Seconds later I went into the commons, and I saw people helping my sister out and who were already holding the kids, and then I heard Mario's voice," Eric continued. "I hugged my sister, and as soon as I saw they were OK, I ran over to see Candace and make sure she was OK."

Like Eric, Candace had taken shelter in a downstairs bathroom. She and some friends were standing outside prior to the tornado, and Candace noticed a wind chime tingling in the wind.

It reminded her of a scene from the movie "Twister."

"About that time a huge flash of lightning struck right in front of us," Candace said. "OK, it's time to go inside."

Candace and five other girls were crouched in the bathroom, praying. A 2-by-4 flew through the shower and lodged into the wall, only six inches above their heads.

When the storm passed, Candace called Eric two or three times. No answer. She did succeed in reaching her father.

"Dad, it's a lot worse than I thought it was going to be," she said. "Just start praying. There are people trapped. There are people dead. There's no way that people are going to walk out of here alive."

Eric, meanwhile, was desperately trying to reach Candace. He ran to the women's complex. En route, he witnessed the destruction in detail and remembers the thought circling in his head: *I bet there must be a hundred people dead here at Union. I can't believe that I'm still alive and all these other people are dead. I should be at the bottom of that pile, because I'm the worst human being at Union University.*

The first person he encountered was Jessica Nelson, who began crying as she tried to explain to him where Candace was.

"When she started crying and saying Candace's name, I thought, *What happened here? Is she pinned under something? Is she still alive?*" Eric said. "That was really horrifying."

But Jessica quickly put Eric at ease.

"No, she's OK," Jessica said. "She's in Blythe 1. I think she's OK."

Eric raced to the room and saw a huge tree that had fallen in front of the door. The front of the building had been ripped open, and Eric could see into the living room.

Inside Candace could hear various people yelling. Then she heard the voice that she most wanted to hear.

"Candace!" Eric yelled as he climbed over the tree.

"I'm in here!" she called back. "I'm OK!"

Eric entered the room and hugged her tightly. The uncertainty was gone. The woman he loved was safe.

"I was really overwhelmed to see her," he said. "She was trying to keep everyone calm. I was so thankful to see her OK. To see her taking care of those girls made me—of course, I already love her—but just appreciate her so much more."

After their reunion Candace, a nursing major, went to the Penick Academic Complex where students were gathering. She and some other nursing students pulled medical supplies from the athletic training room and began treating students with injuries. Some of those students were Eric's roommates.

"They were bleeding all over," Candace said. "They looked like they had been mangled."

But despite appearances, most of those injuries were minor—which gave both Eric and Candace much to think about in the weeks following the tornado.

Why did God protect the Union students? Why would God choose to spare Union the way He did, especially when people died in other places?

"It is a deep mystery," Eric said. "It's not a formula that you can write out. But it is an all-wise and all-powerful God who truly does hold our present and our future and these natural disasters in His hands. They go out at His decree. They don't go to any corner of the universe that He does not decree them to go.

"Because I know that He has power, and because I know that He is good, I can trust Him—that He knows what it takes to conform us to the image of His Son," Eric continued. "He knows what it takes to bring His purposes about. If that meant taking my life, then I must believe that He is good. He is good to us. He is good to His children."

For Candace, the picture of her hunkered down in a bathroom, helpless to do anything about the tornado that raged around her, reminded her of who controls all things.

"That picture of the gospel and how His grace and mercy flowed over Union was a great reminder of how sovereign He is, and how He was in control," she said.

Eric pointed to the words from the hymn, "O Worship the King":

*Frail children of dust, and feeble as frail,*
*In Thee do we trust, nor find Thee to fail.*
*Thy mercies how tender, how firm to the end,*
*Our Maker, Defender, Redeemer and Friend.*

"We are so feeble, and we bring nothing with us to God," Eric said. "It is truly a needy, hands-outstretched relationship to a powerful and wise Father. We do trust that His mercies never fail, and we are so grateful for the goodness He's shown to us."

# John Michael Deakins

Sophomore, Undecided major from Pikeville, Tennessee

*The tornado was huge. I got to my room and shut the door behind me and told everyone that I saw it and it was huge. As soon as we shut the bathroom door and crouched down, the lights went out and the hail started.*

*Within seconds the building was shaking and the ceiling tiles were rattling. I heard Jordan Atwell praying for God to help us and protect us. I found myself praying and holding on to a toilet. I felt like I was going to die and was so helpless. It seemed like an eternity, but the rumbling and glass shattering finally subsided.*

*When we opened the bathroom door all you could hear was screaming and people on cell phones. I proceeded to open my main door only to find rubble and bricks that had to be pushed aside. When I left, I was told by people to head toward PAC (Penick Academic Center) because another super cell was coming. I headed towards the commons only to find myself staring at a pile of debris and a firefighter running across the complex. I saw a girl running towards me crying, and when I looked down her feet were bleeding due to glass.*

*I am thankful to be alive. God had a hand on us, and I am thankful for the mercy He gives and of which I am so undeserving.*

# AARON GILBERT:
# A MEMORIAL OF MERCY

Senior, Covington, Tennessee

*"Therefore these stones will always be a memorial*
*for the Israelites." (Joshua 4:7)*

I f you've ever wondered what it feels like to be inside a soda can as
it's crushed from the outside, ask Aaron Gilbert. He can tell you.

Gilbert, a senior at Union from Covington, Tennessee, was one of
a handful of people inside the Watters men's commons as the tornado
blew it to pieces.

"The building just imploded," Gilbert said. "If you can imagine
being inside a tin can, and it crunching in on you. I could specifically
hear the building crunch and fall in on us."

Gilbert and his roommate Matt Taylor had just bought supper and
taken it back to their room when the tornado sirens sounded. They
didn't even have time to eat their sandwiches.

As a resident assistant, Gilbert had responsibilities to discharge.
He went to the commons to see if Mario Cobo, the residence director,
needed help with anything. Over the next few minutes, Gilbert kept a
close eye on the weather reports and on the darkened skies overhead.
Soon his roommate Matt joined him in the commons.

Aaron remembers hearing the high-speed wind. As the tornado
approached, Gilbert took cover with a few others in a hallway inside
the building. Crouched, with one arm covering himself and one arm
covering the girl sitting next to him, Gilbert rode out the storm as the
building crumbled around him.

"Lord Jesus, have mercy on us," Gilbert prayed. "Protect us."

Through the danger, Gilbert said he never really feared for his life. He felt a supernatural assurance from God that everything was going to be OK.

Indeed, within seconds, the tornado had passed.

"After it was over, I looked up to what used to be the ceiling, and could see the sky," Aaron said. "I kept thinking, I cannot believe this just happened. Then after that, I could hear people screaming. And I started praying for them: 'Please let no one be hurt, have mercy on us, let us find all the people who are hurt. Let no one be dead. Help us get out of this.'"

Taking stock of what had just happened, Gilbert noticed that in his hallway refuge a door jamb had fallen and wedged against the wall, creating a pocket that stopped the ceiling from coming down on him. Just yards away, a metal beam had shot in between two others, missing them by only inches.

Aaron was able to squeeze out of that pocket to a world he no longer recognized.

"It was like a war zone," he recounted. "As soon as I stepped out, we stepped out on what used to be the ceiling. I could feel the shingles."

Then the thought hit him: *Where's Matt?*

"We could hear him screaming," Gilbert said. "He was screaming my name out."

Taylor, unfortunately, had not made it into the hallway in time. And now Gilbert couldn't see him. All he could see was debris piled high.

"Matt?" Aaron called. "Where are you? Can you hear us? Lead us to you!"

Gilbert followed his friend's voice until he found Taylor, covered by two walls of concrete that had fallen on top of him.

"Are you hurt?" Aaron asked. "Can you breathe? Is anything pushing against your lungs?"

"I'm fine. Just get me out of here!" Taylor responded. "How bad am I bleeding?"

Not the easiest of questions for Gilbert to answer, by any means.

"Of course I'm going to lie to him: 'It's not that bad,'" Gilbert said. "You know, he's got blood all over his face."

Then Aaron heard another voice—Danny Song's.

"Aaron? Are you there? Can you hear me? I'm stuck in here. I'm under the couch."

Gilbert joined Danny and reassured him that everything was going to be OK. He told Danny he'd get help.

"One of the most heart-wrenching things he said to me was, 'Don't forget about me,'" Aaron said.

"Don't worry, Danny. I'm not going to forget about you."

And Gilbert didn't. He helped direct emergency workers to the locations where some of the students were trapped. After a while, the firemen let him help move debris off the pile.

As he was working, Aaron got word that another storm cell was quickly approaching. This time, for some reason, he actually was scared for his life. There was nowhere for him to run. He couldn't hide anywhere. *This thing's going to hit us,* Aaron thought, *and I could die right now.*

But then he heard not an audible voice, but the unmistakable nudging of the Holy Spirit asking him, "What do you have to worry about?"

"Well, nothing," Aaron replied.

"Where is your hope? Where is your security?" the Holy Spirit prompted again.

"It's in Christ alone," Gilbert responded. "My only merit is Christ's righteousness. I don't deserve to go to heaven. So if I died right now, I would completely deserve it as a fallen human being. But since Christ has died for me, I get to heaven on His merits, and my sins He has paid for."

"What do you have to worry about, then?" the Holy Spirit challenged him. "Go out there and die for helping people."

Gilbert answered that challenge.

"You're right," he told himself. "I need to 'man up' and get out there and help out. If I get sucked up or die, who cares? My hope is in Christ. And so I was fine. I repented of the selfish thoughts I had. I'm a human being just like everyone else, and everyone else I've talked to has had these thoughts. But when I was out there, I was thinking, save myself. As much as I wanted to stay there with my roommate and help out, as much as I wanted to pass debris and help get it off those guys, your flesh starts rising up, and you say, 'No. Take cover. Go save yourself.'"

He had only a few tiny cuts, and that was it. Yet he found himself complaining that something else might happen to him. He decided that he needed to get over it, and he needed to take those thoughts captive for Christ.

Aaron realized the frailty of his humanity, and he cast himself upon God's mercy. He began to think about what had just taken place, about the power of God that had manifested itself in only a small way, about the way that God had protected him from the storm's ferocity.

"I did not deserve that whatsoever," he said.

He also began to hear from others about the miraculous way in which God had spared them.

Take Mario Cobo, the residence director in the Watters complex, for instance. While Aaron was already crouched in the hallway, he saw Mario running for cover. He thought he saw Mario jump into the hallway. Mario, however, disputes that.

"I didn't leap," Mario said. "I was running to get in and something pushed me. Do you realize if I had been out that door the ceiling would have fallen on top of me? It was almost like something hit me in the back and pushed me in."

Aaron quickly recognized God's hand at work.

"It was like something supernatural just kind of threw him in there—maybe the pressure of wind that God used to shove him in there," Gilbert said.

In the days following the tornado, Aaron had little time to himself. For one thing, he was busy helping with the cleanup efforts. For another, he was inundated with interview requests from the national media—CNN, FOX Radio, ABC's Good Morning America, CBS, even the Canadian Broadcasting Company.

Gilbert thought maybe God was giving him these opportunities to speak openly about His mercy. Aaron took advantage.

"We really felt the hand of God," he said during one interview on CNN. "One thing I noticed is where all the people were trapped, there were little pockets keeping anything from harming them or falling on them. It was definitely the grace of God."

Following the interview, Aaron had all kinds of Facebook messages from other college students he had never met from all over the country:

> "Way to represent Jesus on live TV!"
> "You encouraged me so much."
> "We're praying for our Union friends."

In the days to follow, Gilbert had more time to think through his experiences. He found comfort in such passages as Job 37:11–13:

> "He saturates clouds with moisture; He scatters His
> lightning through them. They swirl about, turning round
> and round at His direction, accomplishing everything
> He commands them over the surface of the inhabited
> world. He causes this to happen for punishment, for His
> land, or for His faithful love."

He thought a lot about God's sovereignty, about trials, about suffering. He recalled how throughout the Old Testament, God constantly reminded the Israelites to remember, remember, remember all that He had done for them.

Gilbert wants to make sure that he heeds that admonition.

"As it gets farther away from the event, because of our human nature and our flesh, things get fuzzier. You soon forget the amazing God who was merciful to you," he said. "I experienced God's mercy first hand, and that changed me a lot."

# Kathryn Borucki

Freshman, Biology (Pre-Med) major from Burlington, Wisconsin

*It was a regular night in the Lex (Union's snack bar)—except for the radio on the counter beside me. When the sirens sounded, we moved to the office in the back. We were sitting in the office, talking and nervously joking, when I heard a loud rumble that seemed to surround us. My boss, Miss Lynn, shouted at us to get in the cooler.*

*She was the last one in, and the suction was already so strong that it turned her completely around and was threatening to drag her and the door away. Someone was laughing giddily, someone was crying, all were calling people's names, trying to determine who all had made it in.*

*When we were told to go to the PAC (Penick Academic Center), I stepped out of the cooler and felt my stomach drop. Above us, the ceiling had begun to cave in, and by the eerily pale light at the end of the hall, I could see ceiling tiles and wires dangling and swinging leisurely.*

*We held each other's hands or shirts and used cell phones as flashlights, and made our slow way to the PAC. I can't forget the mangled cars twisted around one another or the walls and ceilings that were simply . . . gone.*

*God was so good to us in keeping us safe. So much more could have gone wrong that night. So many lives could have been lost. When I see the pictures, I keep getting the feeling that I should have died, and then I remember how very precious life really is. Every day really is a miracle.*

# SARAH SANTIAGO: A TRAIL OF BLOOD

## Senior, Utuado, Puerto Rico

*"For our momentary light affliction is producing for
us an absolutely incomparable eternal weight of glory.
So we do not focus on what is seen, but on what is unseen;
for what is seen is temporary, but what is unseen is eternal."*
*(2 Corinthians 4:17–18)*

The nurse threw her shoe away, and Sarah Santiago was none too pleased.

She knew about the cut on her head, but the gash on her foot had escaped her notice until about an hour after the tornado hit the Union campus. After tracking blood around everywhere—and wondering from whom it was coming—Sarah finally figured out that she was the culprit.

"My shoe is full of blood because I had been walking on it for about an hour and had no clue that I had been hurt," said Santiago, a senior from Puerto Rico. "I had scrapes and bruises all over me for about two weeks. Every day I found a new one."

So when she went to see the nurse, the nurse promptly trashed the shoe.

"And I am really irritated that they threw my shoe away because I am thinking, *You can just rinse it out*," Sarah said. "She's like, 'No, no, this is contaminated. It was disgusting how much blood is in that shoe.'"

"No, I need my shoe," Santiago replied. "I was really attached to

73

my shoe and I needed shoes, because I was going to be barefoot for the rest of the night."

The nurse won that battle, and Santiago—now without shoes—relied on the kindness of friends and strangers alike to carry her across the parking lot littered with shards of metal and jagged glass.

As she rode along, she looked to her right to see cars piled everywhere. On her left she saw what was left of the building that crashed around her earlier that night.

"It was really dark and I couldn't make anything out," Sarah said. "But I just knew there were no buildings standing. I said out loud to the maintenance guy walking beside me, 'I cannot believe . . . How did we make it out of this?'"

He could only answer, "I don't know."

Minutes before the tornado, Sarah was on the phone with her grandfather, telling him that she had passed a test certifying her as a sign language interpreter. Then the sirens sounded.

"I put my phone down on the desk. It was charging," Santiago said. "My room was a mess. I left my laptop on. In retrospect, I think, why did I do this? Why did I not prepare better? What could I have done differently? There's millions of things that I could think of that I would do differently now. And one of those is I would have taken my phone with me because I left my phone on the desk."

Santiago is a resident assistant, so she had the responsibility of going to all the rooms in her building and ordering the residents who lived upstairs to move downstairs in case the tornado hit. Her friend Julie Mitchell, also a resident assistant, was with her as they finished their tasks and headed for the Hurt complex commons, where they were supposed to take cover.

"It was just getting really, really bad, like the winds were getting stronger," Sarah said. "I don't know if this is just me, but I thought glass was shattering around me. I thought I heard the glass shattering. I just could not run fast enough. I thought run, run, run—but I could not move fast enough to get in there.

"We started running toward the commons, and the winds were so strong I couldn't open the door to get in. And I was just thinking *Dear God, this is it. I am not going to be able to get in here.*"

As she strained to open the door, Santiago could only pray, "God, help me!"

God answered her prayer. She forced the door open and bolted inside. Santiago and Mitchell didn't have time to make it to the hallway where they were supposed to go, so they simply clung to each other as the building started falling to pieces.

"When I opened my eyes, I was on the ground," Sarah remembered. "The wind or whatever it was pushed me into the guest bedroom. And I was just lying down. I had stuff all over me. I couldn't move. I was crushed and I couldn't get out by myself. I was laying face down, kind of on my head, and saw my hand in a pool of blood."

She knew she had hurt herself, but she didn't know where.

"Julie, are you OK?" Sarah asked.

"Yes, honey, I am OK. I am OK," Mitchell replied.

Then Julie began praying, "Dear God, dear God, dear God, dear God."

"There was nothing we could do except just pray," Santiago said. "I remember she just said it over and over again: 'Dear God, dear God, help us, help us.'"

Sarah thought about Ema Van Cleave, the residence director for the Hurt complex, who was pregnant.

"Oh no, dear God, protect Ema's baby," Sarah prayed.

God answered that prayer, too. Ema's baby was fine.

Ema's husband Tim came and helped Sarah get up and out of the building.

"The next day I saw the commons, and the commons was totally gone except for the hall where we were," Santiago said. "It was like God had made a little pocket, and He put His hand over us. It was so evident, just looking at the building that the one place—where we were, where there were people—that was the one place that was still standing.

"I truly believe that no matter where we had gone inside the commons, that would have been the only place that was standing. God's hand is so powerful."

Santiago moved to the Penick Academic Complex with most of the other students on campus.

"Every time I saw somebody, it was relief," she said. "I was so happy they were alive, that they were OK. Every time I saw someone from my building, I had no idea what had happened to them. I was happy to see them. And they would say, 'Sarah, thank you for coming and making us go into the bathroom.'"

Santiago escaped that night with only minor cuts and bruises. But she knows it could have been a lot worse—and that wasn't easy for her to think about.

"My world had just been shaken," Sarah said. "Everything was shaken. I just realized nothing is certain. Nothing is certain in this life. I am not certain to have a home tomorrow. I am not certain to have my roommates. I am not certain to have my parents. I am not certain to have my family. All the things that I love, I am not certain to have them. There is nothing certain in this world. I have been told that before, and I have heard it before. It just became really real. I just knew. It's just one of those things that you hear all the time, but I had never experienced it. There is nothing certain in this world, not even my life, not even that I will wake up tomorrow morning. It took a while to deal with the fact that I almost died."

That realization, however—that nearness of death, that hopelessness she felt—led her to cling to the life that she has in Christ, and her complete reliance upon God.

"I hope I can feel that for the rest of my life," she said. "I hope that I will completely rely on God like I did that day, to cry out to God for every single minute of my life. It really shakes your world when you start thinking, *Wow, God really is the only thing I have for certain.*"

Her close call and her loss of possessions—including her shoe—made Sarah re-evaluate the priority of material things in her life. And it caused her to consider in new ways the importance and the beauty of the life to come—a life to be spent in the presence of the God who saved her that night.

"I did not think (the tornado) would affect as much as it has," she said. "I think that by now I would be OK and we wouldn't be thinking about the tornado. It really does hit you at the most unexpected times. It's real hard and I wish it weren't. But I think it's broken me and brought me to depend on Christ completely. God became so many new things to me that week of the tornado. He was my father. He was my friend. He was my provider through others. God has been my provider, and He has been my comforter."

# Megan Johnson

Junior, Nursing major from Goodlettsville, Tennessee

*I was in my room when my roommate and I heard everything. I tried to look out my window and see what I could, but it was dark so there wasn't much to see. As I walked back into the living room, our resident assistant ran by frantically banging on our door, saying the intercoms weren't working, and to get in the bathroom, that it was coming.*

*So at that point we freaked out a little and grabbed our pillows and stuffed animals, and sat in the bathtub. I went to turn off her computer, then I heard a loud noise and walked back into the living room and was turning down the TV when my ears started to pop. Mallory was sitting in the tub still and looked at me with the biggest eyes I've ever seen and screamed at me to get into the bathroom.*

*I ran into the bathroom, sat on the toilet with pillow in hand, and slammed the door. As soon as I was in there, we heard a noise in the living room, the lights went out, and we grabbed each other. The next thing I know Mallory is saying she thinks something is on top of her, so I reach up and open my eyes. I can see the sky through our wall and I felt insulation on top of her. She wasn't hurt and climbed out of the tub, going back for her cell phone.*

*Neither of us had shoes on or a flashlight, so we went searching for those types of things. My bedroom door was slammed shut and stuck, and when I finally got it open I saw my window and bed—and everything was gone but my window was our only way out.*

*When we went back later and were able to see our room, we realized that something had broken through the wall of our bathroom. It was very humbling to see how gracious and merciful God is, even in the midst of something so terrible. It was something I will never forget.*

# KIMBERLY THORNBURY:
# A MASTER OF PREPARATION

## Dean of Students

*"Consider it a great joy, my brothers, whenever you experience various trials, knowing that the testing of your faith produces endurance." (James 1:2–3)*

Kimberly Thornbury wasn't thrilled with the report from her husband Greg prior to the February 5 tornado.

She was at home with their two daughters. Tornado warnings abounded. Sirens blared ominously. Greg, dean of the School of Christian Studies at Union, called to update her on his whereabouts.

"Don't worry," Greg said, "I'm safe in the president's office."

Kimberly's response: "Standing next to the plate glass window in his office?"

It was Kimberly pretending to be upset—because anybody acquainted with her knows that getting her upset is no easy task. She seems to have a smile permanently tattooed on her face.

But Kimberly, Union's dean of students, would soon receive another phone call from Union President David S. Dockery that was certainly no pretending matter. She had heard on the news that a tornado had hit Union, but she had no idea how bad it was.

"I remember Dr. Dockery calling me and saying that the situation looked dire and tragic, that there could be deaths," she said. "I remember the sound of his voice. He's not prone to hyperbole. He's not dramatic. He's not prone to emotion. But I could tell this was something different. This was something serious."

This "something serious" was the rallying cry for Kimberly, a master of preparation, who quickly made her way to campus to do what she does best—caring for the students of Union University in a selfless, sacrificing way.

"This is her calling," Greg said. "She is called to serve the students of this university."

Greg's friend Paul House, when he heard about the tornado, knew that Kimberly would be up to the task.

"I know that Kimberly went to her file drawer and pulled out the scenario for—EF–4 tornado, fifty-one injuries, people trapped under rubble. Here's exactly what you do under that situation," House told Greg.

When she arrived on campus, Kimberly began the process of finding temporary housing for Union's eleven hundred residential students in the homes of faculty and staff members. She told herself that in two hours, she wanted every single student in a bed in a home.

That process kept her occupied at first—so occupied that she hadn't been able to see in detail the extent of the destruction to Union's campus housing. But as she was walking the road with some students, she remembers what she saw when she turned to her right.

"It was the first time I turned right, and I saw the buildings, and I just lost it," she said. "I had no idea. I could never in my wildest dreams imagine that devastation."

One of the most pressing needs Thornbury had to address was contacting parents. But without power on campus, she didn't have access to the university's data management software, and the students' emergency contact cards were in the commons buildings under tons of rubble.

So she quickly drafted students to help her send messages through Facebook and locate phone numbers for all the parents of residential students. All the while, the rain kept pouring down as students were calling her to give her the phone numbers she needed.

"The ink on my paper is getting wet," Thornbury said. "And I'm like, 'Lord, it cannot get wet. I have to know what that number is.'"

She finally took refuge in an ambulance to have a dry space to work and write.

Thornbury quickly discovered that she had to trust God to provide people to help her with the monumental job before her—responsibilities that allowed her to sleep only six hours every third night for more than two weeks.

"You found a willing face, you looked them in the eye, if they looked credible and competent, you would give them assignments," Kimberly said. "You could not wait for someone to say, 'Can I help you?' You just had to assume that the Lord was going to put people in your path who had the skills."

For example, as the emergency phase was ending and Union was making plans for restarting the spring semester, she charged Matt Brunet, Union's director of wellness services, with completely remodeling the student lounge into a coffee house. The conversation went like this: "Matt, we're going to have five hundred more commuting students. Here's $10,000. Redo the lounge so it's welcoming. Got it? OK, great. See you in a couple of weeks."

The pressing time demands didn't give her the luxury of walking people through all the necessary steps they should take. All she could do was give them the outcome or goal and trust them to work it out. The fact that she is a "genius at hiring," according to her husband, also helped in a time of crisis.

"She really does believe in people," Greg said. "She expects great things out of people."

Over the next two weeks, Kimberly had thirty-four teams of people working under her, doing things like retrieving students' belongings from storm-ravaged rooms, assigning new housing to students—and keeping transportation needs in mind for doing so, getting food out of refrigerators in the undamaged rooms so it wouldn't stink when students returned, informing students how to deal with insurance and claims with the Federal Emergency Management Agency, setting up counseling services—and on, and on, and on the list goes.

Along with everything else, Kimberly was heavily involved in the process of designing new student housing to replace the complexes destroyed by the tornado. It was nothing short of a logistical masterpiece—maybe even a logistical miracle.

"The Lord would put ideas into my head," Kimberly said simply.

Maybe that explains why she only slept every third night—because when she would try to rest, she'd keep getting up to scribble notes to herself about different things that needed to be done.

Despite the sleep deprivation, Thornbury stayed sharp and gracious.

"I was in adrenaline mode," she said. "I don't feel like I was crabby. That's another gift of the Lord. I felt clear-headed."

Though physically and emotionally taxing, Kimberly's work load was easy, and her burden was light,

"I think maybe that is the reason why she believes so much in what she is doing—because she herself has experienced what it means to find what God made you to do," Greg said. "She just wants that for everybody. She wants to see them succeed, and she really does delight in it. As much work as it is, it's not work for her."

Kimberly was most impressed with the Union students and how they responded to such an ordeal. For the most part, they were flexible and accommodating.

"I feel like they've risen to the occasion," she said. "When squeezed, we were able to see a lot of Christian virtue and character in our students—which is not only a result of the tornado, but everything that's gone into them before the tornado.

"They are kind and loving and easy to serve," Kimberly continued. "They are very thankful. I honestly think that gratitude is one of the key Christian virtues."

Thornbury thinks the trial by tornado enabled the Union students to put their faith into practice, and even strengthened their faith in the process.

"Faith is the practice of spiritual disciplines, right?" she said. "So I do think there's going to be an increased number of students who practice spiritual disciplines—whether that's going to church, prayer, Scripture memory. And I think they're going to spur one another on, to not just have this ambiguous faith, but this daily faith that's lived out in systematic ways that make you stronger and help you take steps toward Christlikeness."

As for Greg, he sees Kimberly's own Christlikeness in the way she places others above herself.

"I was the president of her fan club before," Greg said, "but I have an entirely new level of appreciation for her now."

# Alyssa Bantz

Sophomore, Nursing major from Fort Pierce, Florida

*I was at a night class in the PAC (Penick Academic Center) when we started getting phone calls about the severity of the storm. Dr. Cooney left at 6:40 p.m. to go check on his family in another part of the PAC, and we made our way to the political science suite, kind of laughing about how all the phone calls were interfering with his lecture.*

*We stayed in the room, kind of antsy, and started to walk around when the walls started quivering and lights went out. All seven of us dove back into the room and under the table— now we REALLY had to get to know our classmates! We huddled to pray, and in a few minutes began getting texts and calls that Union was hit.*

*We stuck together as we emerged into the main hallway of the PAC and began watching students pour in from the dorms. It was at that point that I began to understand the devastation. I guess at that point my story merges with everyone else's in the PAC. The night was broken up with finding information about friends and hugging anyone with a familiar face (which at our school is most everyone). It was chaotic in the halls, yet there was also a sense of peace as I looked around and saw fellow Unionites huddle up to cry out to our Lord, and praise Him for our lives.*

Students making calls after the tornado.

Students moving debris to rescue those who were trapped.

Union President David Dockery surveying the damage on Feb. 5.

Blake Waggoner being treated for injuries.

Firemen and students uncovering debris in the Hurt women's complex.

Jackson firemen working to rescue students from Watters common.

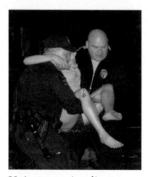
Union security director Bill Young (right) helped carry a female student to safety.

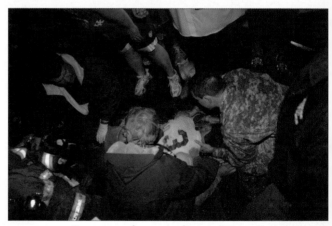
Rescue worker attending to Danny Song (#3).

Mario Cobo (bottom left) watching the rescue operation in the Watters commons.

A Jackson fireman cutting through fallen debris.

Union students carrying Matt Taylor to safety on a stretcher.

In the early morning hours of February 6, dogs went through the wreckage to make sure no students were left behind.

Wreckage from the Watters and Hurt complexes the day after the tornado.

Union personnel evaluated the damage (above) and began the process of recovering students' possessions (right).

Robert Simpson, Union's associate vice president for business and financial services, walking through the wreckage.

Roommates Mattie Trautman and Kristen Schaefer watching their room being demolished.

Kristen Duncan (center) observing the retrieval operation.

Family members attending to Heather Martin, who was overcome with emotion upon returning to campus to see where she had been trapped the night of February 5.

Danny Song (center) looking over the collapsed Watters commons where he was trapped.

Kevin Furniss and his father Bob walking through the Watters common rubble.

Captain Johnny Brantley, of the Jackson Fire Department, greeting Danny Song (left) and Kevin Furniss during a March 14 reunion between Union students and the firemen who rescued them.

Julie Boyer (left) and Heather Martin hugging while they look at the room where they were trapped.

Upside-down cars were a common sight on campus.

Media from all over the country reported on the tornado (above and upper right).

A small sampling of the devastation on campus.

Much of the roof of Jennings Hall was destroyed.

Glass broken on the clock at Miller Tower.

Aerial view of the top of Jennings Hall.

An aerial view of the damage on Union University campus.

Union President David S. Dockery (left) meeting with trustees and the Senior Leadership team in the Chi Omega house, which served as a command center for several days.

Ben Dockery, director of discipleship and spiritual formation, giving instructions to volunteers.

Tennessee Govenor Phil Bredesen (center) speaking to Union faculty, staff, and students.

David Dockery addressing faculty and staff volunteers.

Dockery walking with Tennessee Senator Bob Corker to look at damage.

Sarah Logan (center), Danny Song's girlfriend, giving an interview.

Dockery updating students on the retrieval process.

Dockery at a press conference with Tennessee Governor Phil Bredesen and U.S. Secretary of Homeland Security Michael Chertoff.

Paul Corts, president of the Council for Christian Colleges
and Universities, praying with volunteers.

Union faculty, staff, and community volunteers began the process of retrieving students'
belongings from their heavily damaged rooms.

The retrieval process was a major undertaking that required hundreds of hours of student and volunteer labor.

Eric Smith helping retrieve belongings.

When the retrieval process was complete, students' possessions
filled two gymnasiums and the field house.

Above and below: The clean-up effort
getting underway.

Demolition beginning on the new housing
complexes.

On February 22, just seventeen days after the tornado, Union broke ground on the new student housing complex. Pictured from left to right: President David Dockery, trustees Bill Dement, Bob Campbell, and Harry Smith, and Union administrators Kimberly Thornbury and Gary Carter.

Dockery (left) escorting Tennessee Senator Lamar Alexander around campus.

Construction beginning on the new student housing complex.

The new student housing
buildings went up quickly

Dockery describing plans for the new student housing complex to the Union community.

On February 19 the Union community gathered for a worship service the night before classes resumed. Dockery read Scripture during the service.

Julie Mitchell read Scripture as part of the February 19 worship service. Others involved from right to left: Mario Cobo, Sarah Santiago, and Eric Smith.

Following the worship service on February 19, students gathering at The Jett for a welcome back party. The Jett, formerly the Old English Inn, was donated to Union by Englewood Baptist Church for use as student housing during the rebuilding process.

Classes resuming on February 20, only two weeks after the tornado.

# MATT TAYLOR:
# A GOD OF CONTROL

Junior, Chapel Hill, Tennessee

*"Also, from today on I am He alone, and no one*
*can take anything from My hand. I act, and who*
*can reverse it?" (Isaiah 43:13)*

Looking out the glass door of the Watters commons building into the swirling blackness, Matt Taylor knew he needed to take cover.

He tried running. It didn't work. The tornado blew the door off its hinges, and the force of the wind ensnared him.

"I'm noticing I'm going opposite the direction of where I'm trying to run, and I get lifted up off the floor, picked up off my feet," said Taylor, a Union University junior. "My chest hit the top of the doorframe. That's how high I was."

His legs dangling, Taylor started screaming for his friend Aaron Gilbert.

"Aaron, I'm going to be pulled outside!" Matt yelled. "I need help!"

No sooner did he call for help than the wind stopped for only a second. Taylor dropped to the ground and hit the concrete, gashing the back of his head.

He rolled over and saw blood on his hand. Then he turned to look outside and watched the wind hurl a truck into a tree.

*If I get pulled outside, I'm going to die,* Taylor thought to himself.

The wind was so strong he couldn't stand up, so Matt started crawling toward the closet where he was supposed to be sheltered. He spied a gumball machine. That's got to be drilled to the floor, he thought.

It was drilled to the floor. But that didn't matter. As he grabbed the machine, the wind picked it up and jerked it across his head, cutting him again.

"By that point, I finally just fall back," Matt said. "I'm grabbing my head and then right after that, the loft came down on top of me. And then the other wall came down on top of the loft."

Dazed and disoriented, Taylor lay in shock. He didn't know he was bleeding. He didn't know his head was cracked open. He saw a big-screen TV flying over his head. Then a table. Such commotion should be loud, but he didn't hear any of it.

*I'm already dead,* Taylor thought. *Am I just like a ghost sitting here watching all this unfold?*

He woke up when the building crashed down.

"I was kind of lying on my arm and there was blood on my arm," Matt said. "Still, at this point I didn't feel any pain. I knew that I couldn't move anything from my hips down, but I still had not registered the thought. It was so quiet. I'm like, 'Oh, my gosh! I'm the only one alive.' So I just start praying. I'm praying, 'God, please, just make this quick.' I started feeling pain and I start screaming, 'Is anyone else alive? I need help! I need help really bad!'"

He remembers the dusty, gaseous smell. Then Taylor heard a voice.

"Matt?"

It was Danny Song, another student trapped under the weight of the fallen building. They couldn't see each other, but only a few feet— and a wall—separated them.

"Danny, I think you're hurt really bad because I've got someone else's blood all over me," Matt said.

"I'm not bleeding," Song replied.

All of a sudden, Taylor's head started throbbing. He realized the blood was his own.

"Dude, I think I'm going to bleed to death," Taylor told Danny. "I'm going to pass out because I'm bleeding so badly."

Taylor screamed. But then a new voice reached Matt's ears, bringing hope to his fainting heart.

"Matt, I'm coming!" Aaron shouted. "Where are you?"

"Aaron! I'm over here! I'm over here!" Matt called back.

His friend Aaron—his best friend—found him and started moving debris to get to him. But the slightest movement caused Taylor excruciating pain, so Aaron stopped.

"How bad is it?" Taylor asked. "How do I look?"

"Well, you look OK. You look OK," Aaron said, trying to encourage his friend.

A bypassing student with a flashlight fixed the light on Taylor.

"Oh my gosh. That guy's going to die," the student said.

Not exactly the news that Matt wanted to hear at the moment. So Danny started encouraging the frightened Taylor: "I'm praying for you," Song said. Other friends joined in the encouragement as they waited for help to arrive.

When an emergency worker showed up, he provided news that nobody wanted to hear: Another storm was coming, and they needed to seek shelter.

"What about us?" Matt asked. "You're going to leave us here?"

"Well, we can't get the rescue workers to you right now," the man said. "They're trying to help other people out."

A renewed fear gripped Taylor. But even with another storm heading their way, Gilbert wasn't going anywhere.

"I remember Aaron getting a little frustrated, saying, 'I don't care how bad it gets. We've got to stay and get them out,'" Taylor said.

Finally more rescue workers arrived, but they still couldn't begin working to help Taylor. They needed equipment to remove the debris.

"How long will that take?" Taylor asked frantically.

"We don't know. They're helping other people," came the reply.

"You've got to get me out of here!" Matt said. "If you don't get me out of here, I think I'm going to bleed to death!"

Upon hearing this, Matt thinks their bedside manner kicked in.

"It's only going to be two minutes. Just give us two more minutes," they said.

Half an hour later, and still no equipment in site, Taylor asked again: "You said two minutes. When are you getting me out of here?"

When the necessary help arrived, workers asked Matt to look back at his legs so they would know the extent of his injuries.

Taylor hesitated.

"I'm afraid to, because I'm afraid I'm going to look back and there's going to be something not there, and I'm going to freak out," he told them.

So the workers managed to get to his legs and noticed that the gumball machine across his ankles and a 2-by-4 across his hips were the only thing that kept the concrete from crushing him.

After an hour and fifteen minutes of entrapment, the emergency workers finally freed Taylor. Though he was drifting in and out of consciousness, Matt remembers the last thing he said as he emerged from the rubble: "Danny, they got me out! I'm praying for you! I'll see you at the hospital!"

The hospital was too hectic for Taylor to make connections with Danny. Though each spent the night there, neither was seriously injured. Taylor needed three staples in the top of his head and a couple of stitches in the back of it. Hospital personnel dug glass out of his foot and patched up a cut on his nose. He also required staples in one hip.

The next day Matt returned to the place that he once feared was his tomb.

"We went back in there and just to see the little pockets where everyone was—it was like they were strategically placed there on purpose," he said. "It was definitely amazing to look at. Just even all these metal pipes that shot around us. There were two huge metal pipes right over my head, and it could have easily—I mean, a foot lower and they would have been through my head.

That realization led Matt to a fresh appreciation of God's constant care for him—every day, and not just in times of crisis.

The subsequent days were emotional for him. He found himself crying at random times. Various noises would spark memories. Insomnia gripped him. When he did sleep, the dreams of that night haunted him.

His inability to control his emotions was yet another marker of how dependent he was upon the Lord. It was almost as if God were telling him, "I'm the only person you can come to for peace and closure on what happened."

"We always think that we know how big God is," Matt said. "God had all of our lives right there in the palm of His hands. It was such a reminder for me to see how not in control we are and how much we have to rely on Him. It just really brought back to me how big He is and how in control He is, and I'm not."

# Amber Campagna

Freshman, Nursing major from Memphis, Tennessee

*We got downstairs and there were about eleven other girls there, and we watched the news for a couple of minutes. And then my phone rang around 7:00 p.m. on the dot. All I could understand Trey saying was "I see tornado, get in tub, NOW!" so I told them to get in the tub. We all jumped up, ran into the bathroom, and slammed the door. We all sat down and right when everyone was situated, it hit.*

*The walls started to shake, my ears began to pop, and we were all screaming and crying. The tornado even lifted me off the ground a little. I was terrified the walls would collapse on us. It lasted 35 seconds. I began feeling part of the roof falling on us, and I was terrified. When it was over, we looked up. Still crying, we see the sky. And it begins to rain on us. We were all freezing and crying, not knowing what to do. It was so crowded in the bathroom I began to feel like I was going to pass out because I couldn't breathe.*

*One by one we climb out of the bathroom and walked outside. It looked horrific. It looked like a war zone and that someone had dropped a bomb on our building. People began running, people were bleeding, people were screaming and crying  It was completely terrifying and something I never thought I would experience.*

*I am glad to be alive. I am thankful that the Lord had His hand on Union University. I am thankful no one was killed. From the looks of the pictures, people should have been dead. I honestly don't know how I survived, or how anyone survived. But we did. I did. And all thanks goes to God.*

# HEATHER MARTIN:
# A TUB OF ENTRAPMENT

Junior, Erin, Tennessee

*"We are pressured in every way but not crushed;*
*we are perplexed but not in despair; we are persecuted*
*but not abandoned; we are struck down but not destroyed."*
*(2 Corinthians 4:8–9)*

To Heather Martin, the tornado that changed her life didn't sound like a train. It sounded like a thousand trains.

"The noise was incredible," Heather said. "It was a roar. I felt my legs being pulled up by the force. Then, everything collapsed. A tremendous amount of pressure just kept pressing us. Some of us were screaming. It pushed the breath out of me, so I couldn't scream."

Heather's story may be the most familiar of all the stories from those who experienced the February 5 tornado. Her first-person account, written just a few days after that night, made the e-mail rounds and traveled all over the world.

"I had no idea it was going to be copied and pasted and forwarded all over the place," she said.

In addition, Baptist Press published her first-person account, as did the student newspapers at Union and Western Kentucky University. Charles Colson featured Martin's and Julie Boyer's stories on one of his BreakPoint radio broadcasts.

That's not what Martin intended when she first wrote her story. Three or four days after the tornado, she decided to document her experience to help in the therapy and healing process.

"I just needed to write it for myself," Martin said. "I shut the

91

door and typed for like two and a half hours. My purpose was to get it straight in my mind."

She posted the story on her Facebook profile and e-mailed it to several personal contacts. Within a few days, she was hearing from people in places like Senegal who had received it through e-mail.

Heather has been overwhelmed by the response. Dozens of people have written to thank her for sharing her story. Some of them were strangers who said they had prayed for Union students when they heard about the tornado. That has meant a lot to Heather.

"I think for a lot of people, it was neat for them to see how their prayers had been answered very specifically," she said. "It's been neat to see how the body of Christ has come together. That's been really encouraging to me. It's become very real. It's not just a concept."

Heather's evening on February 5 began an hour and a half before the tornado's strike. She was studying at a local bookstore, but returned to campus when friends called her to express their concern, and to tell her that a dangerous situation was developing.

So she went back to her room as the weather began to change.

"It was stormy but felt like just an ordinary, frustrating tornado drill," Heather said. "I was stressing that I wasn't going to get much studying accomplished."

Her evening would prove to be anything but ordinary. Heather's roommate Suzanne Short burst into their room and yelled, "Get in the tub, now!"

The girls in her room quickly followed Suzanne's order and bolted for the bathroom. Their ears began popping when the pressure changed. They heard the hail slamming into their building. They saw the lights go out.

Martin hadn't quite made it into the bathtub when her room began disintegrating.

"As quickly as it came, it left," she said. "And then there was an eerie silence and darkness. I couldn't see anyone in the tub with me. It was so hard to breathe. A wall pressed down across my back, and my legs hadn't made it into the tub. They were pinned between a wall of debris and the edge of the tub."

As she waited for help to arrive, the gravity of the situation began to grip her. She figured every student on campus was dead or trapped like she was.

*This is where I am going to die,* Heather thought. *No one will ever find us. We will be here for days, and we won't last that long.*

The women in the room accounted for each other and tried to be calming and encouraging to everyone else. Heather knew her legs were pinned, but she wasn't in any pain. Her biggest problem was breathing, which was becoming increasingly difficult.

"I began to think about what my death would be like," she said. "I only had a small pocket of air and my whole body was compressed. I realized I was going to pass out and then I would be with Jesus. That may sound morbid, but it allowed me to not panic about the process of my death."

Then Heather discovered something terrifying. Her dear friend Julie Boyer, who had come to visit her earlier that evening, was underneath her, fighting to breathe. Because of their positioning, anytime Heather tried to move even the slightest, Julie couldn't breathe at all or cried out in anguish.

Said Martin:

> I cannot begin to describe the fear in my heart that this
> precious person was going to die underneath me.
> I prayed aloud. I quoted Scripture. At some point
> I found another friend's hand and she was praying as
> well. After realizing this would most likely be the night
> of my death, I was able to move on and focus on simply
> breathing. At one point I had to tell Julie I was out of
> breath and couldn't pray out loud anymore, but that
> I was still praying in my heart and mind.
>
> This was not me being strong or brave or courageous.
> It was the power of Christ in me. He guided me in my
> thoughts. He helped me to focus on breathing, praying,
> and helping encourage Julie to breathe. The whole
> experience was terrifying, but God was in the midst of
> us. I recall at times just crying out: "God, You are here.
> Give us strength.

Through the turmoil, however, Heather says that God's presence enveloped her. She had "an overwhelming sense of peace" because "we were either going to join Christ in heaven or He was going to sustain us and leave us here on earth for a little while longer."

Firemen arrived quickly and began removing the fifteen feet of rubble on top of Heather and her friends. The rescue process itself was terrifying, she said, because as the workers labored, debris shifted and the pressure on the women increased.

But salvation finally came as the firemen removed the last of the debris. They took Julie to safety.

"Then, a firefighter came and held my torso and head," Martin said. "He kept telling me, 'We're going to get you out of here.' It took a lot of maneuvering and strength on the part of the rescuers because I couldn't feel my legs enough to pull them out myself. A 2-by-4 next to my right knee—between the edge of the tub and mass of debris—kept just enough of the pressure off of my legs so that I didn't completely lose blood flow to my lower extremities. It saved my legs."

Heather sustained only minor injuries—which she says is proof that God was with her that night.

"As I reflect over Tuesday night, I see the Lord," she said. "I cannot explain our survival and the fact that there were no fatalities aside from the fact that God loves us a whole lot and He is not through with us here on earth. The destruction and chaos of Tuesday night is incredible. The amazing power, strength, grace, and love of Jesus Christ is the only explanation I have to offer. In the midst of the chaos and rubble, He knew how each board, each brick, each piece of metal and concrete was placed and He protected us.

Heather admits that she has struggled with her faith in the past. She wondered if she were really a believer. She wondered—if faced with death—what her last thoughts would be.

Now she knows.

"My last thoughts were: God has me," she said. "Either way I am OK. I will either join Him in heaven or He will save me for yet a little while longer here on earth."

The subsequent days weren't always easy for Heather, and the upcoming months cause her to fear sometimes. She'll hear a sound, and it will transport her to that night. Sleep is often elusive.

"However, I find hope in this: God knew, as I lay pinned in that tub, that I would make it out," Heather said. "He is the One responsible for getting me out. Simply put, He is not through with me yet. He already knows what each and every second of the next few weeks and months hold for me, my friends and family. Knowing that gives me hope; it keeps me going. He sustained me through Tuesday night, and He will continue to sustain me in the days that follow."

# Dusty Ruehling

Senior, Social work major from Gruetli-Laager, Tennessee

After finishing homework in the library, I almost returned to my dorm room when I ran into a buddy. We chatted for a few minutes until one of the security guards came down the hallway, telling everyone the storm was on its way and to take cover.

So my friend and I moved back into the middle of the PAC (Penick Academic Center), where a professor ushered several students into the engineering suite. We all sat down and waited, knowing the storm was close. A few people began talking, but I remained quiet and waited. The next few moments are hard to remember; the lights went out, and I heard people screaming and everyone seemed to react. But I remained in the same cross-legged position on the floor. A whoosh burst down the hall, forcefully moving the emergency doors back and knocking over a plant outside the office. Soon everything became quiet again.

Except for the doors and the plant, there seemed to be no signs that anything had happened. Everyone remained still for a second, and outside, I remember someone crying. I stood up and crawled to the entrance, not knowing what to see or expect. The emergency lighting had flashed on, illuminating the once dark surroundings. I didn't know any damage had occurred outside, until my buddy's phone rang. I heard only snippets of the conversation, but by the look on his face, I knew something was wrong. Some of us rushed outside, and I spotted one of the buildings in the Hurt complex. The building was torn apart.

Quickly I joined several people rushing into the complex trying to make certain everyone was OK. At this point, I was running on instincts, checking around through the rubble and knocking on doors, trying to search for survivors.

*After this I want to thank God that everyone is alive and well, and that our school still stands, even though it seems as though we lost so much. I'm excited to see what God has planned for Union in the coming days, and how His glory will shine through this time of trials.*

# MARK AND ANNIE WILSON: A JOURNEY OF UNCERTAINTY

Parents of David Wilson, Chattanooga, Tennessee

*"For He will give His angels orders concerning you,*
*to protect you in all your ways." (Psalm 91:11)*

Text messages between Mark Wilson and his son David were flying across Tennessee.

David, a Union University freshman, was bracing for a tornado. Mark and Annie Wilson were in Chattanooga on the opposite end of the state and wanted to know that their son was safe. They had asked David where he was and who was with him.

"I'm in the Watters commons bathroom with Kevin Bradley and Paul," David replied.

A few minutes later Mark received another message from David: "It just hit us."

"Is everybody OK?" Mark messaged back.

No response.

Mark tried calling a couple of times. No answer. Then David called him.

"Hey Dad. We're trapped. I've got to call 911," David said. And then his phone died.

Mark and Annie had mixed feelings. They had heard from David after the tornado hit, so they knew he could talk.

"And he used the word 'trapped,' which to us said they're stuck in a room somewhere and something's against the door," Mark said. "If he had said, 'We're buried,' it would have been different."

The problem was, David was indeed buried—under more than twenty feet of debris—but just didn't know it at the time. So Mark and Annie were oblivious to the fact that their son was in a situation that nearly cost him his life.

After his last conversation with David, Mark called the Jackson Police Department and Union security to notify them of the whereabouts of David and his friends. He was told crews were already on the way.

"I felt good that people knew where they were and they weren't just going to be there and nobody find them," Mark said. "I still had no idea how bad the damage was, obviously."

Mark and Annie had a friend in Jackson on business, Brian Wennerstrom. When Brian heard about the tornado, he went to campus to check on David.

"I'm standing outside the building where David and his friends are, and there's a hundred people trying to get them out," he told Mark.

"How bad is it?" Mark asked.

"It's really bad," Brian said.

"Do we need to head that way?" Mark asked.

"No question about it," Brian said.

Mark and Annie made arrangements to pick up their other two kids, who were with friends, and travel to Jackson, typically a trip of about four hours.

"There's a list of a hundred things that happened through the night, that you look back at and see the Lord orchestrated every little piece of this," Mark said.

For example, the Wilsons had intended to drive their SUV to Jackson. But when Mark turned the key, the battery was dead. They had to drive their other car instead—which was equipped with a navigation system. That didn't seem like a big deal at the time, but it would prove to be vital.

As the Wilsons started their journey, they began to get calls from friends warning them that they were driving into the path of the massive storm system that had spawned the tornado that struck Union. They called highway patrol to get information about the Interstate.

"The freeway is closed from Nashville all the way to Memphis," they were told. "You'll never get there."

"What about back roads?" Mark asked.

"There are trees down everywhere," highway patrol said. "You'll never get to Jackson tonight. You need to get off the road."

The Wilsons' son was lying under a collapsed building. They weren't about to get off the road.

"You just can't stop when you don't know where your child is," Mark said.

They decided to take the back roads. That's where the car's navigation system came in handy. It guided them along Highway 64, south of Nashville, through towns like Fayetteville and Lawrenceburg.

The drive itself was evidence of God's work, Mark and Annie said. They drove nearly six hours—in the midst of what was supposed to be a horrific storm—and didn't have to turn on their windshield wipers until they were twenty minutes outside of Jackson.

"We never saw a downed tree. No traffic at all," Mark said. "We met only one policeman and told him what has happening. And he said, 'I understand. Be careful.' But we drove really fast, and it still took a long time to get there."

A few days earlier, David's sister Kristen had written out Psalm 91:11 on a card and placed it on the speedometer in the car. As Mark sped toward Jackson, he was constantly reading the words of the psalmist: "For He will give His angels orders concerning you, to protect you in all your ways."

By this time the Wilsons had another friend on site at Union. About every thirty minutes, they got a call from one of their two friends giving them a report about David's status. They were told that the rescue workers could hear David. They knew he was alive.

"We still have this picture that they're all sitting in a room laughing at all the chaos going on around them," Mark said.

More updates came throughout the drive: One student had just walked out. Now there's another one out. One more rescued, carried out by firemen.

Around midnight, Mark's phone rang. It was David.

"I'm coming out and going to the hospital," David said. Then the call ended because a fireman had taken David's phone away from him.

Five minutes later the phone rang again. Again it was David's number calling. Mark answered, expecting to hear David's voice. A fireman was there instead.

"Do you have a son at Union?" the fireman asked. "What's his name? What's your name?"

Mark answered the man's questions.

"I just want you to know that David's alive," the fireman said. "I'm holding his hand and I'll call you when we get him out."

His words jolted Mark and Annie.

"That's the first time we really had an idea that it wasn't what we thought it was," Mark said.

About ten or fifteen minutes later, the fireman called back.

"David's on his way to the hospital," he said. "I promise you he's alive. I put my hand on his chest and I could feel him breathing."

"That really took the air out of our sails," Mark said. "We had no idea how bad it was."

The Wilsons were still about an hour away from Jackson. A few minutes later a nurse from the emergency room called.

"He's talking," the nurse told Mark and Annie. "He gave me your number."

"Is he OK?" Annie asked.

"Well, we're doing everything we can do for him," the nurse said.

That wasn't the answer Mark and Annie wanted to hear. Nor did Mark want to hear the next call he received. It came from one of his friends who had been on the Union campus that night.

"They put David on a ventilator," his friend said. "You know what that means."

"I was literally turning the corner into the hospital at that point, and pretty much decided that they were keeping David alive just for us to tell him good-bye," Mark said.

Mark and Annie parked the car and rushed inside, scared to death that they might not see their son alive again.

"I guess what surprised me the most was how dirty he was," Mark said. "Concrete rocks and stuff in the corners of his eyes, with gunk and crud everywhere, in his hair. He was on a ventilator with his hands tied down."

The surgeon came in and provided the Wilsons with some assurance—at least a little bit of hope. Incredibly, David didn't have any brain damage or any broken bones. He was in respiratory failure, because the lack of blood flow to his legs caused the release of acid into his blood. That's why he was on the ventilator. The second problem was his crushed legs. The third problem was kidney failure.

Annie remembers that first night she spent in the ICU waiting room.

"I honestly could not breathe," she said. "The fear was just overwhelming at times. And then other times you just pray and pray and pray, and you feel peace for just a little while. You know where it comes from, and you cling onto it, but then you'd sit for a little while and you'd start thinking again, and the wave would just rush over you and the panic would just—it would just take your breath away."

For several days the Wilsons didn't know if their son would live.

"I don't know how much of that is just parents being worried as parents, but I mean, his body was so whacked out with so many different things going on," Mark said. "It was probably two weeks before I finally could just say, 'I think he's going to live.'"

David would have a good day, and then he'd regress. Even the good days were a source of concern for Mark and Annie.

"I had a panic attack a few weeks ago just because something really good had happened with David and it panicked me," Annie said. "I thought, *They're going to quit praying. People are going to quit praying.*"

But people didn't stop praying, and Annie would get cards and notes of encouragement at just the right time to let her know that she wasn't alone in her suffering.

And Mark and Annie were suffering. When they weren't worried about David's life, they were worried about his legs. Early on, amputation was not out of the question.

"It takes the will to live out of you," Mark said. "I mean it just sucks the life out of you. There's just no way to describe it, how deep it hurts, and how scared you get."

"And we both—we decided early on—we were like, 'Lord, please, we'll take him in a wheelchair,'" Annie said. "We'll take him any way. Just please let him live. Please let him stay."

God heard their prayers. David's toxin levels diminished. His kidneys began working again. David was transferred to a hospital in Chattanooga and then to a rehabilitation hospital. He was going to make it. The road ahead would be a long one, but David would ultimately recover. He was finally released from the hospital April 11.

"We can let ourselves get absolutely sick with fear and anxiety over what's going to happen next week or next month or six months down the road," Mark said. "But the reality is all we can do is love (our kids) today. That's how all of us are, whether your child's in the hospital or not. You have no control over tomorrow, and I think that's why you choose to be people of faith—because it's all you have."

Though hurting, David himself often provided the encouragement that Mark and Annie needed.

"We would go into his room, and his spirit and the way he would talk, he got us through it," Annie said. "I mean, we would try to be there for him, and he would just say, 'It's going to be OK. I'm alive.'"

Late one night Annie hugged her son as he lay in his hospital bed.

"I am so sorry that you're having to go through this," she told him.

"I'm not," David said.

"Why?" Annie asked.

"Because I think I kind of asked for it," David said.

That's when he told her that he had been praying for God to give him a story to tell—a way for him to testify about God's wondrous work in his life.

"I just sat there in amazement," Annie said. "I told David, 'You've got a story.' He said, 'Yeah, I think I do now. I want to go to schools and churches and tell them what God's done for me.'"

That kind of faith has bolstered the spirits of Mark and Annie through the most difficult days of their lives.

"It's pretty easy," Mark said, "to be parents to a kid like that."

# Katie Moser

Sophomore, Youth ministry major from Memphis, Tennessee

*We had just gotten back from dinner and were hanging out in my room. Like all good parents do, my dad called to tell me to be careful and watch the news because of the bad weather coming through. Like any good college student daughter, I watched the news for about five minutes, and then we started to play Guitar Hero. I had just finished my turn when the sirens went off.*

*We turned the news back on, still joking around and talking about how we should be getting in the bathroom. But did we? No. We were probably the dumbest college students on the planet that night. Then it happened. Everything I'm about to say happened in about 30 seconds.*

*The winds got louder. Mysterious things began to hit our window. Then we knew it was coming. The lights started to flicker in an eerie sort of way. We shut the door and headed for the bathroom. Within the next five seconds, it was over. Then there was a silence that we all described later as eerie and scary.*

*Our front wall was gone. Our indestructible door—that had survived the wrath of our slingshot and soccer ball before—was gone. Once I got out, all I could do was slowly walk out and look around. I still didn't believe that this had happened. To me it was all a dream. But it was real. There were mounds of debris everywhere. There was blood on many people. There were many screaming and crying uncontrollably. In my head there was silence.*

*It cannot be said enough that God's hand was everywhere that night. There is no earthly reason why anyone should be alive who walked out of there. The only explanation I have is the merciful, sovereign, powerful and gentle hand of God Almighty. It was as if God said to the mighty EF–4, "Do your worst. But do not lay a hand on My children." I truly believe that God's hand was holding me and so many others that night. To Him be all the praise, honor, and glory!*

# JASMINE HUANG: A DOOR
# OF COMMUNICATION

Senior, Heifei, China

*"I never stop giving thanks for you as I remember you in my prayers. I pray that the God of our Lord Jesus Christ, the glorious Father, would give you a spirit of wisdom and revelation in the knowledge of Him." (Ephesians 1:16–17)*

She was a fifteen-year-old exchange student from Hefei, China, living in the Bible Belt in Jackson, Tennessee. And though she loved her host family—Wayne and Betty Parrish—Jasmine Huang hated the fact that they made her go to church with them.

"Generally she just did whatever was asked of her," Betty said. "On one occasion she was a little pouty about it. But in general she was pretty cooperative. Most of the time, I would say, she didn't really enjoy it."

Jasmine was, after all, an atheist, just like the rest of her family. She had no use at all for God, and instead was convinced of the merits of her own abilities.

"If I believe that I can do something, I can do it," Huang said. "And that's always my family's philosophy: If you try hard enough, you can do it. Nothing's impossible."

Jasmine, now a nineteen-year-old senior engineering major at Union, has since discovered the truth of that last statement that nothing's impossible. But she now understands it in the context of Luke 1:37: "For nothing will be impossible with God." She has those church services—the ones that she once despised—to thank, in part, for starting her down the path that would lead to her conversion.

105

Ultimately, however, she knows it was God Himself who was responsible for pursuing her and revealing Himself to her through the person of Jesus Christ—just as it was God who protected her during the tornado, giving her a powerful testimony to share with her unbelieving parents.

"If there is one person that brought me to Christ, it has to be God Himself, because looking back, I can see myself doubting Him and trying to make Him prove Himself," Jasmine said. "And time and time again He showed me evidence, one after another. I just can't really say He doesn't exist anymore."

To some it might seem like coincidence. To Christians, however, it looks like God working in specific ways to bring about His purposes in the life of Jasmine Huang. As a high school student in China, all she was concerned about was graduating as quickly as possible. She heard about a foreign exchange program, and her parents encouraged her to pursue it—sometimes against Jasmine's objections. They thought it would be good for her to explore the world and gain an international perspective. Jasmine agreed that the program would indeed offer benefits that she couldn't gain from staying in China, so she enrolled—and ended up at North Side High School in Jackson.

She intended to stay for a year. But after her first semester, a paperwork glitch caused some administrative problems. There was no room for her at the high school for her second semester.

Since she was in Jackson anyway, Huang decided to talk to Carroll Griffin at Union University about the possibility of enrolling in college. Griffin was able to get her into Union's Rising Senior program for a semester, after which she enrolled as a full-time undergraduate student.

Through her exposure to church with the Parrish family, Jasmine began thinking for the first time about what Christianity really meant. She admits it was a long struggle that began before she arrived at Union.

"It's just that nobody really explained to me systematically what Christianity really means and what it means to be a Christian," Huang said.

Enter Huang's first roommates at Union—Abby Carpenter, Katie Watson, and Amanda Atchison. They weren't intimidated by Jasmine's professed atheism, and they weren't about to let that stand in their way of talking to her about Jesus Christ.

"When I came here, it was Katie Watson and my other roommates who chased me down with the Bible and then asked me to read this Scripture and that Scripture," Huang said. "They drove me nuts, but that's really how I got to here, what it really means to be a Christian."

"We knew how she ended up at Union was such an interesting story," Katie said. "We could see God's hand on her. We felt sure that this was so she would hear the gospel and believe. I think that probably fueled our zealousness."

Though their persistence may have annoyed her at first, gradually the testimonies of her roommates and other friends had a lasting effect. She became a Christian right before spring break during her first year at Union.

"I really think God changed my heart because I was so resistant to everything that the preachers preached or my friends told me or Scripture said," Huang said. "I thought everything was just stupid."

To celebrate, Jasmine's roommates bought her a Chinese-English parallel Bible, which she still carries around with her regularly. Inside, they inscribed the words of Ephesians 1:16–17:

> I never stop giving thanks for you as I remember you
> in my prayers. I pray that the God of our Lord Jesus
> Christ, the glorious Father, would give you a spirit of
> wisdom and revelation in the knowledge of Him.

"The Bible was saved in the tornado, and I was so happy," Jasmine said.

She still remembers the phone call she made to her parents to inform them of her conversion. Nervous and fearful of their reaction, Jasmine danced around the topic for a while.

"Mom, you know there are a lot of Christians around here," she said.

"Yes," her mom replied.

"What would you think if I became a Christian?"

The answer surprised Jasmine. Both her parents said it was fine with them if she became a Christian. They figured it was part of American culture, and it was something that Jasmine was doing to fit in. Her mom told her, however, that if church took much of her time, she should drop it—like Christianity was some sort of extracurricular activity.

Though she had embraced Christ, Huang still struggled with her identity as a believer. She could sense her old self and her new self fighting with each other.

"It was probably not until the next summer when I really began to read the Scripture faithfully, and love the Scripture, and believe that I am a Christian and I am saved," she said.

One of her most pressing concerns became the spiritual condition of her parents. Huang has had many conversations with them about their beliefs and about Christianity. Though she admits that her mom is somewhat open to the idea—"She's really trying to read Scripture. She's trying to see what I believe and trying to see if it is true for herself for my sake," Jasmine said—her father remains entrenched in his rejection of Christianity's truth claims.

"I think the one thing that stopped him from becoming a Christian is the same thing that stopped me, just the whole pride issue," Huang said. "He believes if he wants anything hard enough, he can do it. Right now, he's more like, 'This is your thing. I don't mind if you do it, but don't preach it to me. If you preach, I'll listen, but I don't care.'"

Jasmine is praying, however, that the fallout from the February 5 tornado will cause her parents and other family members to be more receptive to the gospel. Like everyone else on campus that night, Huang has her own "Where were you?" story.

She was crammed in the bathroom with fourteen—yes, fourteen—other girls. They heard the walls shaking and the glass breaking, but they didn't realize the storm's severity until they saw a guy coming in with blood on his face.

"That's when we got nervous and smelled gas," Jasmine said. "We sang hymns and prayed. I was smiling the whole time. I was scared in my heart, but it was just really, really encouraging to me—just shocking—to see how peaceful and calm everyone was. I can see they were scared, but they definitely were not terrified. I can see that hope and peace in people, and that really impressed me."

What also impressed Huang was the reaction she saw from so many different people after the tornado—students, faculty, staff, community volunteers—all working together selflessly in a united effort to help those in need. She told her parents about the way everyone pulled together in a time of crisis, unified because of their shared bond in Christ.

"When I was talking with them about the help I got from the community and just what everyone did for me, they just did not understand," Jasmine said.

Her mom, especially, thought maybe people were doing it out of pity or because they would want something in return down the road. But Jasmine told her that was not the case—that people were helping only because they wanted to spread the love of Christ. Such a response made an impact upon her parents.

"I think they are getting to see how Christians act because of Christ," Huang said. "I think that is definitely an eye opener for them."

Prior to the tornado, Jasmine was frustrated with what she called a "gap of communication" with her parents. They were on different wavelengths when it came to priorities and purposes in their lives. But then she told them about the tornado, about how she could have died, about how her life was spared. And the previous barriers she had been experiencing melted away, as she sensed anew her parents' concern for her well-being.

"That brings warmth to my heart because we are still connected," Jasmine said.

It also brought her a renewed sense of urgency in communicating the gospel to the two people she loves the most. She relayed to them the accounts of how people responded to the tornado. She told them about the peace and comfort that God had provided her during a time of disaster and calamity. She told her mom how important it is to have a God upon whom to depend in such times.

"I think that showed her more of what I really believe and showed her more that Christianity is not just an activity or interest, but really what my life depends on," Jasmine said. "It's who I am."

# Lauren Laster

Freshman, Political science major from Olive Branch, Mississippi

*I had been planning on a birthday dinner at Olive Garden with friends that night. My mom had called around 6:00 p.m., telling us to hold off until the tornado warnings passed. When the sirens started, my roommates and I immediately went downstairs and joined our neighbors in their bathroom.*

*There was about ten minutes of small talk before my roommate suddenly said to shut the bathroom door. Two seconds later the electricity went out, our ears popped and we heard the violent wind breaking windows. I don't remember the sounds of the destruction, thankfully, but mostly remember pleading with the Lord to keep His angels around us.*

*Once the eerie silence after the storm settled in, we waited in the bathroom for about 20 minutes before someone knocked on the door telling us to move to the commons. The most distinct memory of the night came when I left that dorm, turned around, and saw for the first time the hole where our living room had been. I still didn't realize the amount of devastation until the next morning. The organized chaos of that night still amazes me and makes me even more thankful for our God's amazing power and order. It is definitely a birthday I will never forget.*

# MARIO COBO:
# A SENSE OF RELIEF

### Residence director, Watters Complex

*"So because of Christ, I am pleased in weaknesses, in insults, in catastrophes, in persecutions, and in pressures. For when I am weak, then I am strong." (2 Corinthians 12:10)*

As Mario Cobo was running for cover, the roof collapsed just inches behind him. In fact, the force of the blow actually propelled him into the hallway where others were huddled for safety.

But his worst fear wasn't that he wouldn't make it. His worst fear was that his four-year-old son Isaac was behind him.

"I realized that night, I really thought I had probably lost my son," Cobo said. "Every time I remember, I just want to lie down on the ground and be thankful. I could have lost my whole family there, and God has spared them."

Cobo, a native of Ecuador, was the residence director for the Watters men's housing complex at Union University when the tornado hit. That means he was responsible not only for the welfare of the three hundred-plus men who lived in the complex, but for the welfare of his wife Rebecca and their two children, Isaac, four, and Sofia, two, as well. The Cobo family lived in the Watters commons building that was leveled during the storm.

He had been monitoring the weather all day, and when the sirens started sounding, began ordering students to safety. That didn't always go as smoothly as he would have liked.

"Of course, they are young students and a lot of them think they

113

probably are invincible and indestructible," Cobo said. "They actually wanted to see the storm, wanted to be outside."

Others only wanted to play ping pong in the commons building.

"What are you guys doing?" Cobo chided them. "You're playing ping pong and the alarms are going off."

"Come on, Mario," one student objected. "Come on, man."

"I was like, 'You come on. Let's get in the bathroom right now,'" Cobo said.

Cobo continued corralling people to safety until the tornado was upon him. His wife and children were sheltered in a hallway along with a few others, and Mario was en route to join them.

"When I turned around, it was just a big explosion," he said. "It was not a train sound. It was just a big explosion, but by that time, everything came down. It looks like the roof cracked in two. It came down and it hit me on the back. And actually, it was a good thing, because it hit me and pushed me into the hallway."

But for a split second, the terrorizing thought hit Cobo. Was Isaac following him around when he was making his rounds? Was Isaac behind him when the ceiling caved in?

"So I start yelling for Isaac," Mario said. "And then—that was the best ever—Rebecca, my wife, said, 'He's here. He's fine. Just get us out of here.'"

Cobo had never been more scared in his life.

"I knew everything came down, and I thought my boy was down there. And that was just—oh, man—just to think about it, I get . . ." and his voice trailed off.

But like dozens of students on campus that night, Cobo's family was safely sheltered in a pocket of protection with a building lying in ruins all around them. Other students, however, didn't make it into the hallway in time. Danny Song and Matt Taylor were not far behind Cobo when the ceiling collapsed on them.

After the storm had passed, Cobo stepped out to sights and sounds he'll never forget. The first thing he noticed was that he was standing on the roof—or what used to be the roof. Students were wailing. Some were yelling, "I'm trapped! I'm trapped!" Others were running from their rooms down to the commons to check on Mario and his family.

"That was also very touching, because I saw a lot of the students coming out and looking for Isaac and Sofia," Cobo said. "They knew the kids were in there and the commons were the most devastated."

The students' selflessness also struck Cobo. They didn't emerge from their rooms thinking, "I'm OK. Time to get out of here." No, they were running into buildings that could have collapsed at any second looking for their fellow students.

"They were not really worrying about themselves," Mario said.

He saw Blake Waggoner running around trying to help, with blood pouring from his head.

"Are you OK?" Mario asked him.

"Yeah, yeah I'm OK," Blake replied. "Where's everybody? How can we help? What can we do?"

Mario helped his family out of their hideaway, and Rebecca took the kids to a safe place. Then Mario had to get to work. He had students who needed to be rescued, and emergency workers who needed to know where they were.

"We have two right here," he told rescue workers, pointing to where Danny Song and Matt Taylor lay trapped beneath debris.

Then he thought about the guys in the bathroom.

"Look, we cannot hear them. We cannot see them. But I know there are seven guys right here," he told a fireman.

Mario watched as rescue workers pulled student after student from the rubble. Even though some of them had been trapped for hours and languished in pain, the first thing they asked when freed was about Mario and his family.

"They were thinking about Isaac and Sofia," Cobo said. "They knew they were in the commons, and they cannot even move, and they are still thinking about other people—and especially my family. So that was, again, really touching."

After more than five hours of digging, rescue workers pulled the last guy—Jason Kaspar—from the building. As they loaded him onto a stretcher, Jason gave Mario a thumbs-up. The load on Mario's shoulders was suddenly a lot lighter.

Gene Fant, Union's dean of the College of Arts and Sciences, remembers seeing Cobo at 1 a.m. staring into the rubble.

"His quick thinking and brave efforts helped save those young men who had been trapped," Fant said. "Despite losing everything, he selflessly cared for students who were, in a very real sense, a part of his own family. I thought about my own children and hoped that, should they ever be in a similar crisis, they would be cared for in the same way."

Over the next few days Cobo tried to salvage as much as he could from his family's apartment that lay in shambles. His family lost a lot—pictures, videos, other sentimental items. On one trip through his apartment, however, he found his wife's wedding ring. The second time through, some soccer players found her engagement ring.

"That was awesome," Mario said.

He was also able to recover Isaac's favorite toy sheep—which helped soften the blow to the young child.

"I really thought they wouldn't remember much, but my little boy, I think he remembers everything," Cobo said. "He can tell you all the details. He can remember people. He can remember Matt being trapped. He can remember Danny. And, of course, they are all his really good friends."

The transition hasn't been easy for the Cobo family. Their home was destroyed. Many of their possessions were lost. But despite the calamity, Mario watched in amazement as God's people loved him and cared for his family in their hour of need.

"They've just given us cars and things like that," he said. "It's been almost worth it to go through something like that, just to see God's love through people. I know we're going to miss a lot of the things that we lost, but we just have gained so much faith in people.

"There is no doubt that God's grace was upon Union, plus He had a bigger purpose that we cannot see, and God was just working throughout the disaster to show people that we depend upon Him," Mario continued. "Just sometimes we have to get to our knees, I guess. The Word says that when we are weak, we are strong, and everybody had been really brought to their knees to make us realize that our strength is in God and we depend on Him for everything."

# Allison Craft

Freshman, Mathematics and secondary education major

from Collierville, Tennessee

*Jazz band practice required me to be in Jennings Hall that night. Around 6:45 p.m., Dr. McClune, my band director, told us to stop playing and stay in Jennings because there was a tornado warning. I had just gotten off the phone with a friend when all of a sudden, Dr. McClune yelled for us to get in the student lounge. As soon as he closed the door, the ground shook, the power went out, and my ears felt like they were literally going to burst out of my head. I was huddled in a chair curled up in a little ball. I knew the tornado had hit.*

*Never before have I felt like I wouldn't see my friends or family again. I knew we were in the safest building, but I was just waiting for the ceiling to collapse and trap us under three stories of concrete. I was so scared. After a while we walked across the lawn to White Hall. Those that had survived the dorms collapsing had been sent over to the PAC (Penick Academic Center) and White Hall. People were everywhere screaming, crying, vomiting, calling their loved ones. I had no idea what destruction the tornado had caused. I had not yet been able to see the dorms.*

*It really struck me about how bad it was when a guy walked in, shirtless and bloody from head to waist. It looked like he had been trying to help either himself or others out of the rubble. His hands were wrapped up like he had been reaching through glass or debris. Later on, half a dozen of my friends walked in, those that I was really worried about. We embraced and cried a little. Everyone then was separated into different classrooms. About sixty of us were in one classroom. We began reading Scripture and singing songs and praying. It was a very peaceful experience.*

*The next morning we saw exactly what the campus looked like. It was absolutely the worst thing I've ever seen. By the* power of God, the most devastating tornado that night went through Union's campus and no one was killed. When I think back, I see God's presence hovering over the campus that night and His gentle hand was guiding every single student to where they were supposed to be. As my biology professor, Dr. Huggins, said, "Right before the tornado hit, I believe that the angels landed and spread their wings over each and every student." That is so true. God is so good.

# TORI GILL:
# A PLEADING OF LOVE

## Junior, Union City, Tennessee

*"We know that all things work together for the good of those
who love God: those who are called according to His purpose."*
*(Romans 8:28)*

Tori Gill sat with her family in the back row of the balcony at
Second Baptist Church in Union City, Tennessee.

"I hate it," Tori said. "I hate sitting in the very back, because I feel
like I'm missing everything. But that's where we sit."

Her dad, Brock Gill, was on the end of the row. He had been the
focus of Tori's prayers for eight years. She desperately wanted to see
him come to know the Lord who had changed her life.

But she was beginning to consider the situation hopeless. Time
and again, when the pastor gave the invitation, her dad refused to
budge from his spot at the end of the pew.

"I honestly had become numb to the altar call, as far as thinking
about Dad," Tori said. "It just wasn't going to happen."

Tori had become a Christian when she was twelve. She had
been raised in a Christian environment, with her mom Stacie and her
grandparents.

"My parents had me when they were really young, so they decided
it would be best for my grandparents and my mom to be the main
caregivers," Tori said. "My dad really didn't come into my life until a
later time."

Indeed Stacie was only sixteen and still a high school student
when Tori was born. Her dad was not a big part of her life for a few

years. But when Tori was in third grade, her mom and her dad got back together and married.

"That's when the father-daughter relationship kind of came into play," she said.

Her father did not have any kind of Christian upbringing. And he had no interest in going to church with Tori and her mom. But by this time, Tori's Christian foundation was well established. She knew the Bible stories. She knew who Jesus was.

"But it wasn't until I was twelve that I actually realized the price that Jesus paid for me," Tori said. "I kind of felt the magnitude of that. That's when I asked Christ into my life."

Discipleship came during her high school years as a member of the youth group at Second Baptist Church. During her sophomore year, she went on her first mission trip. During that trip she realized that her passion for life was children. She knew for the first time that she wanted to teach. And she rededicated her life to Christ.

As college loomed, Tori expected to attend the University of Tennessee at Martin. But her youth minister and his wife, both Union graduates, persuaded her to go to Union. She knew that she'd have to trust God to provide the financial means for her to do so.

"My mom and I worked like dogs—scholarship after scholarship after scholarship," Tori said. "Dad had said, 'Tori, you're going to have to find another school because it's just not going to happen.'"

But Tori was undeterred.

"Yes it is, because I feel like this is where I'm supposed to go," she told him.

Sure enough, the necessary scholarships came through, and Tori found herself at Union. When she left for college, her dad began attending church somewhat regularly with her mom. Tori's church family knew his story, because Tori had requested prayer for him many times.

It was only natural for her to do so, because she was praying for him nearly every day. On February 5, she didn't realize how close her prayers were to being answered.

That day Tori got out of class about 3:30 p.m. and went back to her room to take a nap. Her roommates were gone, and she didn't set an alarm. She awoke around 6:30 p.m., cooked dinner, and watched some TV before going to a friend's room a few minutes before the tornado struck.

She had been sitting in a chair under a window. She got up to get some shoes, took two steps, and saw the window shatter. Tori and the other girls shot into the bathroom to take cover.

Her family, meanwhile, had been watching the weather reports on TV. They heard a report that Union had been hit.

"I called Tori immediately and couldn't get her," Brock said. "We had just talked to her about 30 minutes before, right before the storm hit. That worried me. She's always got her cell phone on her."

Brock even offered a silent prayer: *Please, God, just make sure she's OK.*

After the storm had passed, the girls emerged from the bathroom, rattled and frightened, but unscathed. They looked outside and saw the devastation around them. Tori still didn't have any shoes on, so she grabbed the closest ones she could find then left the room with her friends to find a place of safety.

"Here I am in these humongous shoes, holding hands, running through the parking lot," she said.

She spent the night with a friend, and finally made contact with her parents.

"My heart was relieved," Brock said.

The next day her parents came to get Tori and help her retrieve her belongings from her room, where she had not yet returned.

"All my stuff was pretty much OK, but the top floor had pretty much collapsed on mine," Tori said. "If I'd have been in my bed and not awakened, that's where it collapsed. Right on top of my bed."

She knew it was not a coincidence that she had awakened when she did.

"I didn't just do that by myself," she said. "I had no doubt that night that my alarm clock was God. He made me get up. I don't have a doubt."

Tori said her father's visit to campus that day had an impact upon him. Robert Simpson, Union's associate vice president for business and financial services, escorted the Gills to Tori's car and engaged her dad in conversation.

"God provided last night," Simpson told Brock. "And we're so thankful."

The "God talk" continued throughout the rest of the week after Tori returned home. Church members came by to visit and bring gifts.

"So many times, I feel like, Dad was exposed to God," Tori said. "Because on a daily basis, he didn't get a lot of that conversation. I cried all week, because I was so thankful for those people who stepped up."

That brings us back to the Sunday when Tori was sitting with her family in church. It was the first Sunday after the tornado. And this Sunday, things were different.

"I was sitting there with my eyes closed," Tori recalled. "As soon as I opened my eyes, my dad is down there already. I remember thinking, *Wait a minute, is that my dad?*"

Sure enough, it was. And Tori knew what that meant. Her dad was surrendering his life to Christ.

"I was almost in complete shock that it was happening," Tori said. "So here I am almost running down the balcony steps. I got down there, and I was bawling by that time. Dad was still talking to the pastor."

She waited patiently until their conversation finished. Then she sat down next to her father on the front row. He hugged her as she cried.

"This week just hit me hard," Brock said.

"I've been praying for so long," Tori replied. "I've been praying for so long."

"It felt so good to say that to Dad, because I don't know if I've ever told him that I've been praying for him," Tori said.

Tori knows that the way God protected her during the tornado had an impact upon her dad.

"I think it was the first time that Dad was able to see how God protects His children," she said. "And he was able to see also the hope that comes after it—that I'm not going through depression, as I think some people might—because I know where I stand with God. I know that since He did provide for me that He has more things to do with me. I think that's what got to him."

Brock echoed that analysis.

"Once I heard Tori's voice on the cell phone, I was convinced right then: Somebody's taking care of her," he said. "I saw what happened to the campus and could not believe that she survived—or anybody survived. I think that was the turning point for me. Somebody was watching over her."

That Sunday night Brock was baptized at the church and is now a member there. Though thrilled that her father had made a public profession of faith in Christ, Tori knew the days ahead would tell the story.

*I hope this is real,* she thought. *I hope it wasn't just an emotional time and he just made this decision because of that.*

But as she watched her dad's life in the weeks ahead, she became convinced that his conversion was genuine.

For example, the next week Brock was flipping through the channels on the TV, when Tori said something unwholesome came up on the channel he was watching. Brock purposely decided to change channels.

"To me, that spoke volumes," Tori said. "I thought, *Whoa. That isn't Dad.*"

Then there was the night when her mom awakened at 2 a.m., and Brock wasn't in bed yet. Stacie walked out to the living room to check on him and found him reading the Bible.

Tori has seen the changes in his life in other ways as well.

"He's happier," she said. "He's more loving. I feel like I can approach him more. I feel like I can go to him with things, and I think it's going to open up the communication about spiritual things a lot more."

Brock himself knows his life is different.

"I feel loved, and not just from my family," he said. "I believe that I'm loved by a superior being. I know my family loves me, but I know it's more than my family. I'm loved by my Christian family at church.

"I especially feel more love from Tori, because she knows that she'll now see me in heaven," he continued. "That really hits my heart pretty good."

Tori has been able to hit some hearts herself as she's told her story to her friends at Union.

"It's been so great to touch people on campus," she said. "I've made almost everyone cry that I've talked to."

As she reflects on the events of February 5, Tori can now see the way God used the crisis for His glory. For her, that meant the salvation of her father.

"I truly believe that nothing but good has come from this tornado," she said. "For me personally, if it took me losing everything in my dorm for this to happen, then I would do it ten times."

# Jonathan Moore

Junior, Business management major from Covington, Tennessee

*As I sat in the bathroom in the McAfee commons, we passed the time reading and watching funny YouTube videos. Just then the lights flashed out, the pressure dropped, and an immediate rumble shook the building. The sounds of shattering glass and screaming people filled the air. A few minutes later thirty girls came pouring into the building because there was a gas leak in one of the dorms.*

*I had no idea that the damage was so severe until we were evacuated to White Hall. As I walked out the door of the commons, I stood in amazement at the horrific scene. It looked like the exodus of Egypt as students picked their way through rubble, toppled cars, and power lines. The first floor of White Hall was an amazing environment. In the midst of tears, screams, and the yells of medics, there was praying, Scripture reading, and sweet reunions. The powerful sounds of "Amazing Grace" and "How Great Thou Art" filled the building.*

*I couldn't find my fiancée Courtney, and I started getting really worried. I asked everybody I knew if they had seen her, and finally, I saw her at the other end of the hall. I have never seen a more beautiful sight!*

*I cannot say how grateful I am to the people who cared for us and have given us so much. Through this whole experience I have felt God's hand on every inch. I feel my faith has been strengthened in this time of struggle. I have joy in Christ because He is unshakable. As I have spent the last few days working on campus in various capacities, I have seen firsthand the outpouring of help from the community and the resolve of the students, faculty, and staff to recover and rebuild. Together in Christ we will stand.*

# GEORGE GUTHRIE:
# A MINISTRY OF CARE

Benjamin W. Perry Professor of Bible

*"The hidden things belong to the* LORD *our God, but the
revealed things belong to us and our children forever, so that we
may follow all the words of this law." (Deuteronomy 29:29)*

His role may have been one of the most difficult tasks in the
days following the tornado. But for George Guthrie, a Christian
studies professor at Union, his job may also have been among the
most rewarding.

Guthrie was one of the faculty members charged with the care of
the students—and their families—who had been hospitalized by the
tornado. While that certainly meant spending hours at the hospital
counseling the injured students, praying with them, and comforting
their parents, it also involved some other assignments—like tracking
down sentimental possessions from dorm rooms that were now in
shambles.

Kevin Furniss, for instance, wanted his laptop, a bin of sermon
notes he had been taking in church since the eighth grade and a col-
lage of photos and other memorabilia from an eight-baseball-stadium-
road-trip he and his friends had taken. The awning outside Furniss'
room had collapsed and blocked the door, so Guthrie got down on all
fours to crawl into the room. A few minutes later he emerged from the
room with all three items secure.

And although he wasn't the one to find it, Guthrie was able to
deliver to Cheryl Propst, who grew up in Africa as the daughter of

missionaries, a painting she had made of an African village near her home.

For Guthrie, it was simply part of the job of caring for those in need—something that accompanies a true sense of Christian community.

"If we really are being a biblical community the way that we need to, that means that you not only try to meet the spiritual needs that are there," Guthrie said. "You also try to meet the practical needs, because it's holistic. So, it was really kind of a tapestry of things that we were doing to try to meet the specific needs."

Union University Provost Carla Sanderson said Guthrie was representative of Union faculty and staff members who served students in heroic ways by helping to retrieve possessions from storm-battered dorm rooms.

"At daybreak on the morning after the storm, it was clearly evident that the homes of eight hundred students were lying exposed," Sanderson said. "We had to do something. Obviously, some student belongings were buried deep in rubble, while others were basically intact rooms with roofs and walls blown off."

Union faculty and staff worked with local law enforcement officials, the Tennessee National Guard, and structural engineers in devising a plan to enter every room to retrieve students' belongings, sometimes from rooms that were structurally unsafe.

"For four and a half days, these volunteers served, retrieving passports, wallets, family treasures, computers, clothing, textbooks, and on and on, labeling and bagging each item for student retrieval," Sanderson said. "The belongings filled two gyms and the field house."

Sanderson said the most touching story she heard was about a student named Sarah.

"Sarah had come to campus to ask that someone retrieve her money from her room," Sanderson said. "A faculty member came out of the rubble and handed Sarah an envelope which she quickly opened. But she shook her head and said, 'No, I need you to go back in. This money is my tithe. I need my spending money.'"

On February 5 Guthrie's care for the Union University students—specifically for the injured students and their families—began from his own home in Medina, Tennessee, about ten miles from the Union campus. He and his family were monitoring the local news and tracking the path of the tornado. At one point, it was heading directly toward them. But then it veered east. He realized what that meant.

"That's got to be going right through Union," Guthrie told his wife Pat. "So we just started praying. I remember that night praying that God would hide our students under the shadow of His wing, that He would protect them."

Guthrie heard conflicting reports over the next few hours about the severity of the damage to the Union campus. As the smoke cleared through the night and early the next morning, Guthrie's dean, Greg Thornbury, asked him to go and visit the students in the hospital.

"From that point through about the next five or six days I was probably at the hospital four or five hours a day, just making the rounds," Guthrie said. "I feel like I was very blessed because God gave me a very focused role that I could do and that was to try to care very specifically for the needs of those families who were in this crisis situation."

Guthrie's job soon became more varied and eventually involved such duties as collecting gift cards for the students in the hospital, securing free meals for their parents at places like Outback, Olive Garden, and the Flatiron Grill, talking to hospital administrators about insurance concerns, dealing with FEMA issues—pretty much anything and everything that he could do to help those families at the hospital who were in need.

Through it all, Guthrie got to see up close the faith in God that these families demonstrated.

"The families were amazing," Guthrie said. "They were strong. They needed to talk. They were getting exhausted, but their faith was unwavering. With every family, it was very powerful to see their calmness and their faith in the face of their kids being hurt very badly."

David and Candy Kelley were one of those families. Their son Matt, a sophomore from Somerville, Tennessee, was one of the Union students most seriously injured in the tornado. He spent several weeks in the hospital. David said that Guthrie had called or visited every single day during Matt's hospital stay.

"He's been great," David said about Guthrie. "He's come to the hospital. He's prayed with us. He's just been great. He's gone out of his way, and I really appreciate that."

Guthrie's ministry to the Kelley family also provided the opportunity for a reunion between him and David.

"I didn't realize that George was at Union until all this took place," David said. "George and I played Little League baseball together. I hadn't talked to him in twenty years. We've had a reunion, and he's just kind of taken care of us. He's made sure we've been taken care of in every way."

David had to visit campus a couple of times to identify some of Matt's belongings, and Guthrie took him around to help with that process. He even took David to the site where Matt was trapped. As David stood, stared, and wondered at God's protection, Guthrie was at his side.

"It was hard," David said. "I'm glad that I did. There's no way I can imagine what (Matt) went through. But it made me feel good to see it. I've known all along that there's no way he could have survived without the Lord protecting him. After I saw where he was, it just confirmed that. It's a miracle that he got through it, that all those guys got through that with their lives."

Reflecting upon the destruction caused by the tornado—and the miracle of everyone's survival—has led Guthrie to some theological conclusions that he appreciates more now than ever.

First is the conclusion that God is powerful and good, and He does indeed protect His people at times, even when He chooses not to protect others.

"We live in a fallen world in which bad things happen," Guthrie said. "The created order is longing for the redemption of the sons of God, Paul says. The fact that we live in a fallen world means there is no guarantee. God does not promise to intervene every time evil or something bad happens, but He graciously does intervene. And a right response is to praise Him, thank Him, to see His hand at work. Just because God did not spare everyone's life in West Tennessee or the South does not mean God did not spare the lives of our students and people here on campus."

Second, Guthrie thinks trying to ascertain God's motives— why He did this, why He didn't do that—is a tricky business. For Christians confronting such issues, he says it's better instead to dwell upon what we do know about God.

And what we do know is that this world is not perfect. It is marred by sin and is a corrupted vestige of God's original creation. And that even if God had chosen not to shelter Union University, He would still be deserving of praise.

"Death is not the worst thing that can happen to a believer," he said. "So, I think it has kind of deepened that sense that we can rest in God's providential care and look to Him in trust, and then try to respond appropriately."

Third is the understanding that God can use the evil in the world—the tragedies, the disasters, the hurt, and the pain—to bring great glory to Himself. Even the crucifixion of Christ was both the darkest and the brightest day in human history.

"I think in some ways this moment in Union's history will be both the darkest day and the brightest day in the years to come," Guthrie said. "Because we have seen the community of faith manifested, I think providentially we are going to see the campus actually move forward in a dynamic way. At the same time, it is appropriate to grieve what is lost in the situation, and the hurt and the damage that has been done. But we do both. We grieve and we celebrate in light of who God is and His good gifts and His providential care."

And fourth is the appreciation that a day is coming when God will eradicate all sorrow and death and suffering, inaugurating His eternal kingdom of perfection for those who have trusted in Christ.

"I think that Christian vision of things is the only hopeful one, that we really do have a Lord who is in control, but at the same time we don't see the manifestation of that yet," Guthrie said. "Amazingly God is able to turn tragedies inside out to make us more of what He wants us to be and look like."

As he watched the old student housing complexes being demolished—the ones that stood on campus for nearly thirty-five years and housed him as a college student—Guthrie certainly felt a twinge of sadness. He knows there's a nostalgia that he'll never get to experience again. He'll never be able to take his kids to his old dorm room and show them where he lived.

"But it's overshadowed strongly by excitement about the future," he said. "I love progress and seeing things develop. I think it's exciting to see the transformation that's going to take place physically on campus. I think in some ways, that just matches the character that has already been manifested through the whole event."

# Drew Head

## Sophomore, Theology major from Lexington, Kentucky

*You know that intense feeling in your ears you get when you ride an airplane? Well, that stuffy noise filled our ears as the tornado came closer to my room. The kitchen window shattered. Pieces of glass were hitting me. One even cut my forehead! I then fell to the ground with eight other guys, and we put a mattress over us to protect us.*

*I remember at that precise moment looking up at the ceiling and seeing the roof turn orange. Bright orange. It was at that moment that I realized that this was a very serious matter and people's lives were in danger. After that had ended, we waited a second and then went outside to assess the damage, along with all the men from Watters living complex. Think back, if you have seen it, to any scene in the movie Twister, where a town was destroyed. That's what our side of the campus looked like. Concrete was everywhere, we were stepping over power lines and our commons had collapsed with people inside.*

*Here is where the fun begins. Mass pandemonium broke loose as students began to search for friends, and firefighters and staff rushed up and down the hallways (trying to maintain order). Then I saw a miraculous thing. I saw unity at Union like I have never seen before in my entire life. It is expected for times of tragedy, but it was such natural unity and care for one another that I knew God was working and stirring hearts of people that night.*

# BLAKE WAGGONER:
# A SYMBOL OF HEROISM

Senior, Franklin, Tennessee

*"Hallelujah! Salvation, glory, and power belong to*
*our God, because His judgments are true and righteous."*
*(Revelation 19:1–2)*

Tornado sirens will forever have a new meaning for Blake Waggoner. On February 5, 2008, they were simply a blaring nuisance to him.

Like many on campus, the engineering major didn't take the tornado warnings as seriously as he could have. Seriously enough to make room in their downstairs apartment for their upstairs neighbors? Yes. But seriously enough to cram into a bathroom with nine other guys before the storm's arrival? No. Blake had been through the drills before, and nothing had ever happened. Why should that night have been any different?

That would soon change in a big way. Sitting in his living room watching the weather reports on TV, he started to feel his ears pop. Then the living room window exploded, the door caved in, the lights went off, and stuff started blowing around everywhere.

"As soon as that window shattered, we all just sort of made a line for the bathroom and all nine or ten of us were able to fit in there pretty quickly," Waggoner said. "So we made sure everyone was in there and tried to shut the door."

Easier said than done, however, as the ceiling had started caving in, and the bathroom door wouldn't close until the guys shoved the ceiling back up.

Blake had felt some of the wind-tossed debris hitting him, but it wasn't until he got into the bathroom that he realized he was cut. He only noticed it then because he felt the blood dripping on him—from his ear, running down his neck, and also on his hand.

"So I grabbed a towel and at first started to wrap it around my hand, but then someone else was bleeding, so we gave them the towel," Waggoner said. "I took my shirt off and wrapped it around my hand, to try and kind of stop up that bleeding."

His injuries would later require medical attention, as glass was embedded in his ear and his hand—fifteen stitches in his leg, five in his ear, three in his hand. And like so many others on Union's campus that night will testify, inches made all the difference. Had the cut in his ear been an inch or two lower, it would have been in his neck.

"It could have been bad news for me," Blake said.

After about thirty seconds or a minute, the storm had passed, and Blake and his bathroom-crammed roommates decided they needed to pray. Blake led them in prayer, thanking God for His protection during the storm, and praying for the safety for everyone else—because Blake did not yet know how badly battered the campus was. Figuring that out didn't take long.

Blake emerged from the bathroom with little trouble. Then he looked into his bedroom to see the walls gone.

"Then I walk out my door and out to the commons, and the commons is just a pile of rubble," he said. "And I'm like, 'Oh, man. People could be dead here.'"

Blake started calling for people and could hear the muffled responses coming from underneath the rubble. The next few minutes were chaotic, as he and other friends tried to determine where people were trapped, if they were hurt and how they could be reached. Common sense told him that he couldn't do much to help.

"It's just bad to try and start to dig people out when there is that much debris on top of them, because you could cause it to collapse and it might make it worse," Waggoner said.

Nonetheless, with blood pouring down his face, hands and leg, the barefooted Waggoner stayed close by, trying to help in any way he could. He didn't leave until emergency workers forced him to seek medical attention.

"You had Blake Waggoner walking around with his shirt off," said Union senior Aaron Gilbert. "He had cut his hand really bad, had a cut behind his ear and needed about fifteen stitches on his shin. And he was walking around, helping out, making sure everyone was OK. He just tied his shirt around his hand. He was forced to leave because he was injured. I'm pretty sure he would have stayed a lot longer."

Blake's selflessness didn't escape the notice of Union President David S. Dockery.

"Blake was symbolic of the heroes that night—hurt himself, but mostly wanting to help others around him," Dockery said.

Waggoner found his way to the paramedics, who removed the glass from his ear and his hand. He went to the hospital for his stitches, and then stayed the night at a professor's house before heading home to Franklin, Tennessee, the next day.

That gave Blake a chance to reflect more fully on what had transpired. He realized how close he was to death, but he also began to appreciate even more the assurance he had in Christ—and that an eternity in heaven awaits him when his life on earth is finished. Still, that realization doesn't erase the fear of the moment entirely.

"I don't want to over-spiritualize it like it wasn't scary, because it was still frightening," Waggoner said. "It's one thing to look back and analyze theologically, but when you are in that moment, it's scary."

He didn't stay home for long, however. A day later Blake came back to Jackson to begin helping with the recovery effort. To him, it would have been miserable to have stayed home and dwelt on the events of February 5, when he could have been helping those in need.

"I think that one reason I did want to come back and help and get involved was because it would be sort of overwhelming to try and sort through all that by yourself," he said.

For Blake, helping was part of the healing. It also gave him the opportunity to speak to a broader audience about God's protection for the students, and about the gospel. In an interview with the Wyoming *Torrington Telegram*, Blake was quoted as saying, "If you saw the complex and knew it was populated, you would have to assume people died. We are in awe of God's hand of protection over the students." In an interview with video producers from FedEx, he also had the opportunity to present the gospel.

It's important to seize such opportunities when they are presented, because the gospel provides an answer to the questions many people are asking. Some of those questions, Blake even asked himself in the days after the tornado.

"We can't just sit back in our Union circle here and say we thank God for our protection here," he said. "Yes, thank God for that and give Him praise for that. But what about the people who did lose their sons, and their mothers, and their grandparents? That has sort of been in the back of my mind. How do you deal with that?"

Furthermore, how would people at Union have responded if God had removed His hand of protection, even in just a few cases?

Blake doesn't have all the answers, but he does know that God's ways are just even if He had allowed people at Union to die. He is certain what he would have seen in response from the Union community had that been the case.

"I feel confident people would still have been able to praise God throughout it," Waggoner said. "I am sure there would have been even more intense spiritual struggle, especially for the parents and close friends, sort of asking 'Why?'—the natural question. But I do feel like the overall response of the campus and community would still have been one of faith and even thanksgiving."

# Rachael Moore

Junior, English major from Dyersburg, Tennessee

*I will never forget what it looked like when we stepped out of our room. Everything was so eerie. There were flashes of lightning in the sky and flashes of lights from ambulances and fire trucks illuminating the horrible devastation of what used to be our home. We all just huddled together as we walked and cried.*

*When we stepped out past our building, I looked down towards Wingo and Jelks and saw many guys I knew amidst firefighters and policemen carrying unconscious girls out from the rubble. I just knew lots of people were dead—including our friends. I saw them loading people onto stretchers in ambulances, and I started thinking about all the funerals I was going to have to go to.*

*As we were walking, I was looking back towards the areas that used to be our commons, and I saw how much damage the tornado had done. I started crying because everything we used to have was gone. My boyfriend Mark started calling me and trying to find where I was. Eventually I found him outside White Hall, and I felt a lot better. I walked into White Hall to find my roommates, and there were people all down the halls being treated by nursing students. I began to see the faces of many of my friends, and with every face I was more grateful. Every time I hugged someone I just didn't want to let them go.*

*My dad got to campus in record time and took me home to Dyersburg. We stayed there until morning when we could get up and go survey the damage on campus. Before we left, though, I turned on the TV to find Union everywhere on the news—only to find out everyone had survived! It was a miracle. Mark and I had talked to most of our friends before our phones died, and we knew they were fine. We were finally able to sleep a little after we knew Danny Song wasn't trapped anymore, but I still thought other people were dead. It's a complete, utter miracle. God's protection was on all of us on February 5, and He deserves all the glory. Without Him, none of us could have survived.*

# JULIE MITCHELL:
# A HOPE OF RESCUE

## Senior, Scottsdale, Arizona

*"So don't worry, saying, 'What will we eat?' or 'What will we drink?' or 'What will we wear?' For the idolaters eagerly seek all these things, and your heavenly Father knows that you need them. But seek first the kingdom of God and His righteousness, and all these things will be provided for you."*
*(Matthew 6:31–33)*

For Julie Mitchell it was like the cavalry had arrived.
    She remembers creeping from the building where she had ridden out the storm. After seeing it decimated and lying in heaps all around her, she wondered how many people had actually survived.

From her perspective it couldn't have been many. But then she saw a welcome sight. Even now the memory is a vivid one.

"Guys started pouring into the complex, over the rubble, too," said Mitchell, a senior from Scottsdale, Arizona. "The one exit that we all eventually walked through, there was a lot of debris. Guys just kept coming in yelling, 'Who needs help? Who needs help?'

"I wanted a rescuer in that time, to be honest," she continued. "Jesus Christ rescued us, but it was also a blessing to see someone— other human beings, lots of them. Also, that gave me hope."

Julie was one of the resident assistants charged with getting students into the lower-level bathrooms in the minutes preceding the tornado's arrival. Her job requires her to be serious about such matters, but Julie often gets razzed for being a little too diligent.

That night, however, Julie's diligence saved lives. She was in the Hurt women's complex commons building when she got a report that one downstairs room had nearly twenty girls in it. Her director, Ema Van Cleave, told her to go and move some of them to different rooms. Another RA, Sarah Santiago, accompanied Julie.

"Sarah says I was a little bit harsh, which is probably true, but I was just kind of fed up," Mitchell recalled. "I was like, 'Come on, this might get serious,' and we separated them."

By the time they finished that task, they knew the tornado was bearing down on them. Julie attributes that sense of foreboding to God's urging.

"Sarah, run, run, run!" Julie ordered Santiago, as they raced back to the commons building.

"Every step we took, it was like the force of wind and the force of the rain was heightened every second," Mitchell said.

She and Sarah barely made it back into the commons when the tornado began pounding the building apart. Others in the commons were able to take shelter in a hallway, but Julie and Sarah didn't have time to join the others.

"Sarah and I just grabbed onto each other," Julie said. "Because we were standing, we were thrown around the corner into the adjoining room. I remember there was probably a minute or two where we were just still. And then we started to move and Ema screamed, 'Don't move! Don't move!' and I remembered when I opened my eyes I saw the sky above me.

"I didn't hear a train," she continued. "It happened so fast and then it was over. It happened so fast. I mean, it wasn't even raining when I looked up from the ground. It was just quiet. I love roller coasters, and I really felt like I was just on a ride. I really do."

She remembers sitting up and seeing Sarah with blood all over her face. They weren't trapped, so they made their way through the debris and out of the building. Julie will never forget the sights that unfolded before her.

"It was like a bomb had been dropped," she said. "It was chaotic. You couldn't see very well. It had kind of that eerie haze. There was a grayish light in the sky. It wasn't pitch black. I remember seeing some piece of furniture in the tree when we first walked out and was like, 'What the heck has happened?'"

The light of approaching fire trucks brought Julie a sense of relief, as she then moved from the collapsed building to another building on campus where students gathered following the storm.

Many students were understandably upset and shaken. Julie was able to minister specifically to one young man:

"Something that was really special to me was I was able to pray with someone," she said. "A guy that had been in one of my classes was just really frantic and I think he was having a panic attack. People were just gathered around looking at him and so I was looking for something to do because I guess that is just how I would respond. I just needed to do something.

"So I just said, 'All we can do is pray right now,'" she continued. "I was able to pray with him, and this was a guy I didn't necessarily feel close to at all. Just to see him really, really vulnerable. It was really humbling."

A few minutes later nursing professor Molly Wright—a good friend of Julie's from church—arrived to take Julie and several of her friends home for the night. Wright had been trying to call Julie, to no avail. Naturally she was worried.

"I went in the chapel door, and it was dark. I couldn't see anybody," Wright recalled. "I went down the hall. There were people everywhere. There were people yelling and people crying."

Wright eventually found Julie, and the two shared a tearful reunion. Then they walked with the other girls across campus back to Wright's car. At Wright's house, Julie nursed her wounds, then fell asleep in the arms of her roommate, Ashton Bruce.

"I was hit in the back with some debris so I had a bruised rib," Julie said. "I was really tightly wrapped, so my roommate and one of my best friends, Ashton, just held me and played with my hair until I fell asleep. I don't think she slept very much."

In the days to follow, Julie thought a lot about how she—as a Christian—should respond to the tragedy she had just experienced. She knew she and other students would have a platform to talk about their faith in God, and she wanted to be sure she took advantage of those opportunities.

*In times of tragedy, people often thank God even though they are not followers of Christ,* Julie thought. *What is going to set us apart and make our stories different from what people read all the time?*

She answered those questions by thinking about what her response would have been if people had died.

"This is very much not finalized in my mind," she said. "I am still very much talking to God about it and struggling with it. But I think, the Lord is the only holy One—and whatever He chooses to allow or He brings, He is our rock and it doesn't matter what happens."

Julie did one interview with a TV station in Paducah, Kentucky, and another with Trace Gallagher of FOX News.

"I really don't have a big story for you," she told Gallagher. "God was looking out for us, and we were protected."

That protection has prompted Mitchell to depend upon the Lord more than she ever has in her life—on a daily basis.

"I think a month ago I was worried about what I was going to do for the rest of my life," she said. "And now I am just worried about what I am going to do tomorrow."

# DAVID DOCKERY:
# A PILLAR OF STRENGTH

## Union University President

*"God is our refuge and strength, a helper who is always
found in times of trouble." (Psalm 46:1)*

David S. Dockery, president of Union University, is a tornado
veteran.

In November 2002 a twister hit the Union campus and caused
about $2 million in damage. Less than six months later, in May 2003,
another tornado came through Jackson. Though the brunt of the
storm missed Union, the campus still sustained broken windows and
water damage.

He thought those two storms would prepare him for what he
would see on the night of February 5, 2008, after he heard reports that
Union had been the target for yet another whirlwind.

He was wrong.

Dockery had eaten dinner with Gene Fant, dean of the College
of Arts and Sciences, and Greg Thornbury, dean of the School of
Christian Studies. The three men were in Dockery's office when the
tornado hit.

"My cell phone started ringing," Dockery said. "People said the
residence life area has been hit. I grabbed an umbrella and we headed
for the residence life facility. As I was going, I was bracing to see,
once again, what I had seen at midnight, November 9, 2002—only to
get out there and see devastation ten, fifteen, or twenty times worse.
Everywhere I looked, walls were coming down. Students were stream-
ing out of the dorms wondering what to do."

145

The news only got worse, as Dockery soon received word that several students were trapped under fallen buildings. He called 911, only to find out that rescue workers were already on the way.

So began the night that Dockery knows will be the defining moment of his life.

"The rest of my life will be lived post-February 5," he said.

The night, however, was just beginning. Dockery set up a temporary command center near the dormitories where he could communicate with emergency personnel, administrators, and students. Around 8 p.m., Marty Clements, director of the local Emergency Management Agency, told Dockery he needed to move to the police station in downtown Jackson, where he could better focus on the challenges before him and better communicate with the police and fire departments, hospital, EMA, and the media.

"I hated to not be here on campus, but everybody had seen me here for the first hour," Dockery said. "I couldn't do very much, but my presence indicated that things were quasi-under control."

In the days after the tornado, Dockery received two or three hundred e-mails from students thanking him for his presence that night.

"Every time I was on campus, I saw you," wrote sophomore Kristin Dutt in an e-mail to Dockery. "Every time I saw a set of pictures, I saw you. Every time I watched the news or read a report, I saw you or heard your name, and witnessed you giving all the glory to the Lord."

At the police station Dockery spent much of his time talking to Union Provost Carla Sanderson, who was at the hospital, and Dean of Students Kimberly Thornbury, who was trying to get the students off campus.

Over the next five hours, reports trickled in as one-by-one, the trapped students were rescued. But as time passed, Dockery began receiving mixed messages about some of those trapped students. At one point, he was told that the final two students were probably dead.

"We kept calm," he said. "We kept the most positive word coming out that we could, and that turned out to be the right word. God protected us that night. Those students' lives were spared, and each one was able to be rescued."

Dockery returned to the Union campus about 2 a.m., after the last trapped student had been rescued, and watched as emergency personnel brought in dogs to sniff through the rubble for anyone who might have been left behind.

"We started praying," Dockery said. "We thought we had everybody off, but we knew we had to do this to make sure there was nobody buried under all the fallen rubble."

The dogs found nobody. Every student was accounted for. Dockery went home at 3:30 a.m., took a shower, and spent time in prayer before going back to campus.

"I asked God for help beyond anything He had ever given me before," Dockery said.

"The first thirty-six hours were the most challenging thirty-six hours of my life," he continued. "My theology about angels and my theology about the providence of God carried me through that first thirty-six hours. I have a deep sense of God's providence. It moved from theoretical to reality. It was all we had to hold onto.

"As I looked at the rubble late Tuesday night, and especially when the sun came up on Wednesday morning, I said, 'There's no way we didn't have two hundred people die.' I'm convinced—nobody will ever convince me otherwise—that God's angels were unleashed to come as ministering spirits to His people that night and to protect those students in the most precarious situations. I'm confident that's what happened."

But while the students were alive, Dockery wasn't convinced that Union University was. At one point, as he surveyed the damage in the early morning hours, he entertained thoughts that not only was the spring semester a lost cause, but that Union University as a whole might be as well.

"That was my worst fear—that the devastation was such that we may not be able to recover, at least in a timely fashion," he said. "That was always my prayer, that God would somehow give us wisdom to figure out how to restart the semester. We knew we had to save the semester for the seniors, and then for others as well."

The questions facing Dockery and other Union administrators were overwhelming. How do you even think about starting classes when 70 percent of your student housing is gone? When one major academic building has no roof and is flooded throughout? When other buildings had also sustained significant damage?

"I knew it didn't depend on me," Dockery said. "I was trusting in God and His providence, and we have a team of people—but I knew that everybody was looking to me for answers and guidance. I knew that wrong decisions would only compound our challenges. We had one chance to try to get every decision right from the get-go.

"We prayed that God would protect us from making wrong decisions, that He would give us wisdom beyond our abilities and our experience," he continued. "That was our constant prayer. I knew we were going to have to live without sleep and that we would be tired, and that we had to have some supernatural energy."

Indeed Dockery didn't sleep for almost seventy-two hours following the tornado.

"Refreshing showers and the Psalms carried me through," he said. "I spent more time reading the Psalms in those first two weeks than I've ever spent reading the Psalms in my life. They were life-givers. They gave me life and hope. The psalmist expressed my cries to God in ways that I was having a hard time doing. The assurance that God is our refuge and our strength and our hope was all I had to cling to. It gave not only personal assurance, but it gave me a vocabulary to communicate to others at a time when people were looking for hope."

Dockery gathered with Union's Senior Leadership Team at 9 a.m. on February 6 in the Chi Omega house to begin making plans. They faced several pressing needs, such as assessing the damage, figuring out how to save the spring semester, deciding how to start the cleanup effort and determining how to communicate most effectively to students, parents, faculty, and staff.

His leadership during Union's hour of crisis was instrumental in the university's recovery.

"He was optimistic. He was clear. He was wise. He was informative and helpful," said Kimberly Thornbury, Union's dean of students. "He constantly framed the discussion to keep us on track and to keep our priorities in order. He started every meeting and ended every meeting with prayer, even when it didn't seem like we had a moment to spare, and everything was time-sensitive. The room right next door was burgeoning with people needing answers. He was calm, and he would always pray, and pray at length.

"And he always wanted us to pray for the injured students," Kimberly continued, "something that he has continued to emphasize in every meeting since February 5."

Greg Thornbury said that through the events of February 5, Dockery demonstrated that God's grace is real in his life.

"I don't have words to describe how amazing David Dockery was from the very first minute," Thornbury said. "This would have broken any lesser man. They'd have cracked under the pressure. But in the most adverse of circumstances, minute by minute, hour by hour, he exuded the grace that David Dockery is legendary for.

"It's not an act," Thornbury continued. "He is the real deal, 100 percent authentic, Christian original."

Dockery and the Senior Leadership Team created a five-phase plan that would guide the university through the challenges before it. The first phase was a forty-eight-hour plan to get Union through the crisis period. The second phase shifted Union's attention to students and how to go about salvaging their belongings.

"We soon realized that students had left campus as they were," Dockery said. "They didn't have their wallets. They didn't have their keys. They didn't have their drivers' licenses. They didn't have credit cards. They didn't have their international green cards. We needed to find that kind of stuff."

The next phase involved restarting the spring semester, which Union did on February 20, only two weeks after the tornado. Dockery still shakes his head when he thinks about it.

"The ability to restart the spring semester was one of the most amazing things that I've ever witnessed," he said. "All of our colleagues in higher education are still marveling that we figured out a way to start the semester. I mean, we had to move eight hundred students off campus. We had to refund over $2 million in housing payments. We had to relocate entire departments—music, Christian studies, communication arts. This was not an easy thing. We had to revise the spring semester in a way that did not lose any time from class and would allow us to graduate on time.

"Our academic leaders—led by Provost Carla Sanderson—deserve medals of honor, in the same way that our student life team deserves hero badges for what they did for and with our students on February 5 and 6."

Subsequent phases of the Union plan addressed long-term rebuilding and communication efforts. Hour by hour, day by day, the university operated out of that plan. And it worked—thanks largely to the abundant support Union received from external sources. Two days after classes resumed, Union broke ground on two new student housing complexes.

In typical fashion Dockery was quick to recognize others for that success as well—most notably Gary Carter, Union's senior vice president for business and financial services.

"Gary worked closely with Kimberly Thornbury to help us think about replacing the residential life buildings and with other campus leaders and trustees in the repairing of the other buildings," Dockery said. "Gary has managed every project, provided oversight for the assessment processes and helped to carry out the insurance negotiations, while serving as the point person on all matters regarding finances. His ability to support his colleagues and keep others informed of our needs and challenges has been the glue to recovery process."

In the days after the tornado, thousands of volunteers poured onto the Union campus to help with the relief effort. The city and county offered unwavering support. Other help came from unexpected places, like when Englewood Baptist Church in Jackson offered to turn the operation of its hotel, the Old English Inn, over to Union to use for student housing.

"When they told us about the hotel, I knew we could figure out a way to house the students," Dockery said. "And if we could house the students and come up with a schedule, we could start the semester back."

Financially the university was in a predicament as well. That's why Dockery said the action from the LifeWay Christian Resources board of trustees was so significant. LifeWay President Thom Rainer—one of Dockery's closest friends—called him the night of February 11 and told him that the LifeWay board had unanimously voted to make a $350,000 donation to Union's recovery efforts.

"We want to walk alongside our brothers and sisters in Christ at Union University," Rainer told Dockery during a conference call with the LifeWay trustees. "We thank God that lives were spared, and we thank God for your incredible leadership. You have stood tall at a time when the pressure would have crushed other leaders."

Dockery said LifeWay's generosity was crucial for Union's survival.

"I don't think that can be overstated," Dockery said. "That set the bar for gifts."

Other sizeable donations quickly followed from the Southern Baptist Convention Executive Committee, Tennessee Baptist Convention, GuideStone Financial Resources, Bellevue Baptist Church in Cordova, Tennessee, Southern Baptist Theological Seminary, and many others.

"I don't think you can ever see those as anything other than God sending us symbols of hope—that He was going to touch hearts in all different spheres and sectors of our relationships to come and help us," Dockery said. "But we still face a minimum of $12 to $15 million in the next six or eight months, or we're still in some difficult waters. There are incredible markers of hope that God is with us. He is going to get us there."

That confidence began just a few hours after the tornado. As Dockery looked at the fallen buildings, he said God put a thought into his mind: Out of the rubble, God would bring renewal.

"I live with that sense of hope," Dockery said. "God's going to bring spiritual renewal to the lives of students. The kind of work He's doing in my life I know He's doing in the lives of dozens of others, if not hundreds of others. We're going to rebuild this campus, and it's going to be better."

The Sunday after the tornado, Dockery attended church at Englewood Baptist Church. One of the songs that day was "Blessed Be the Name of the Lord." Tears streamed down Dockery's face as he struggled through the song.

"Trying to sing those words—'He gives and takes away, He gives and takes away'—was very, very hard to do," Dockery said. "I had sung that song fifty times before. But singing it with the reality that everything can be taken away in seconds brought that to a completely new awareness of how fragile life is and how totally, utterly dependent I am—we are—on God and His grace and His providential care each and every day."

Two weeks after the tornado, at exactly 7:02 p.m.—the time the tornado hit the campus—Union students, faculty, and staff gathered in the G.M. Savage Memorial Chapel on campus for the first time post-tornado. That night, the day before classes were to begin again, that same song echoed throughout the chapel.

"Blessed be your name, on the road marked with suffering," the Union community sang. "You give and take away, but my heart will choose to say, 'Blessed be your name.'"

In his remarks that night, Dockery used Psalm 84 to relate Union's past and future to the prayers of the psalmist, who longed for the place where he had met the living God. Dockery emphasized to Union students that it was the psalmist's displacement from that special location that created within him a longing for God and the things of God.

"It may well be that our current situation may result in a new yearning and hunger for God and the things of God for many of us here tonight," Dockery said.

And although the pre-February 5 Union University was irretrievable, Dockery expressed his hope for a new future.

"Here, the impossible can become possible," Dockery said in comparing Union's situation with that of the psalmist. "Affliction can point us to joy. Ashes can become beauty, hardship can be turned to rejoicing, rubble can become renewal, and weakness can be transformed into strength. We can, by God's grace, become an oasis of hope to others across this campus."

As Dockery reflected upon the events of February 5 and the following weeks, he recognized that his life will no longer be the same.

"I'm more tired," he said. "I've reached points where I've never been this tired before."

He also has a greater appreciation for the people with whom he works.

"To watch them work, to watch them carry out their service has been joyful to behold," Dockery said.

But most importantly, he has a renewed sense of God in his life.

"I live with an awareness of God's presence, His providence, His abilities to preserve life and to provide for us, in ways that I've never experienced before," Dockery said. "When you look and see how close we came to total disaster, and at the same time how we were spared from that, you just have to cry out, 'Thanks be to God.'"

# CONCLUSION

*"I will say to the LORD, 'My refuge and my fortress,
my God, in whom I trust.'" (Psalm 91:2)*

The stories of God stepping into human affairs and acting providentially at Union University don't stop there. Hundreds of others
have their own accounts of how God protected them that night, and
how God has worked in their lives since then.

Take Brittany White, a freshman from Littleton, Colorado.
Brittany called her dad Neal just after the tornado came through. Her
roommates were scared and sobbing.

"I could barely hear my dad, because they were crying so loud,"
Brittany said.

As she reported on the incident to her father, she was about to
hang up.

"Can you put me on speaker phone?" Neal asked. "I'll pray for
you guys."

Brittany punched a button on her phone and held it up for everyone in her room to hear, as Neal prayed for them.

"He prayed over us specifically, over Union and over Jackson
as a whole—even though we didn't know at that point exactly what
had happened and how much damage there was," Brittany said. "He
prayed that God's will would be done and that we would see Him
through whatever happened."

Brittany knows without a doubt that God answered her dad's prayer.

"It was traumatizing, but it was so obvious that God was watching over us as the tornado came," she said. "I would never wish disaster like this upon anyone else, but I wish everyone could experience God in the way I've experienced God since then, and in the way I think Union's experienced God."

For Stephanie Clark, assistant coach of the Union women's basketball team, the tornado provided needed perspective for her and for the entire team.

"We talk a lot about basketball being a game," Clark said. "It's a platform, and something we can use to make God's name great. It's a gift of our life, and it's not the end-all and be-all. It's a game, when the rubber meets the road. And if you're not playing to glorify God, then it's worthless."

As the Lady Bulldogs cruised through an undefeated regular season—winning thirty-five straight games before losing in the national semifinals, the team became a rallying point on a campus that needed something to cheer about.

While it was basketball for the fans, it was more than that for Clark.

"It got to be a ministry for us, because that was one of the first things that was normal in our campus life," she said.

"Normal" is not something that Matt Kelley will experience for quite some time. The Union sophomore from Somerville, Tennessee, was one of the guys trapped in Watters commons, and sustained some of the most serious injuries—primarily to his legs. He spent several weeks in intensive care and faces a grueling rehabilitation as he learns to use his legs once again.

But despite the circumstances, Kelley is grateful to be alive. At times, he didn't think he would be.

"It was so hard to breathe," he said. "There were times when I didn't know if I was going to make it or not. I prayed a lot. I had to have faith in God that I was going to make it."

Another prayer answered. Another life spared.

"I guess God just has something in store for me that's special," Matt said.

Megan Romella Evans, a first-semester freshman from Atlanta, Georgia, can echo that sentiment. Megan had been a student at Union for only a week when she encountered the tornado February 5. Not only did she survive that, but she survived a car wreck on February 17 just before she returned to campus for class.

"I could have died, twice," she said. "God, you have me alive, apparently, for some really good reason."

These stories—and the others you've encountered in this book—are like threads in a tapestry. Individually they can be appreciated on a small scale. But our gracious Father in heaven is truly a master weaver who has taken these separate accounts and fused them into a grand design of providence, displayed for the world to see.

My hope and prayer is that by reading these stories, you have had a renewed sense of God's involvement and activity in human lives, of God's providence, of His mercy, and of His love. Of course, the most dramatic example of all these things came in the person of Jesus Christ—the way, the truth, and the life.

Like the Israelites who erected a stone memorial to celebrate God's parting of the Jordan River, these stories will be our memorial to celebrate God's protection from the mighty whirlwind. We truly can affirm the words of the great hymn, "O God Our Help In Ages Past," written by Isaac Watts:

> O God our help in ages past,
> Our hope for years to come,
> Our shelter from the stormy blast,
> And our eternal home.

# AFTERWORD

George H. Guthrie, Benjamin W. Perry Professor of Bible,

Union University

Vance Havner, a colorful writer and speaker from a generation ago, once noted, "Any man touched by Jesus Christ is good publicity for the gospel."[1] The word *gospel* simply means "good news." In the ancient world, the word was used, for instance, of a messenger who brought good news to an individual, a family, a city, or the population as a whole. The good news might have been the announcement of victory in battle, a wedding, or the birth of a child. Thus, it was a word associated with joy and excitement.

As the dust began to clear on February 6, the day after the tornado, we heard the "good news" that no one at Union had been killed in the storm, in spite of initial projections by emergency workers that there would be one hundred fatalities. Needless to say, we were excited and very, very thankful. The way that our leaders, our faculty and staff, and our students were protected from the storm and have responded to the destruction caused by the tornado really has been "good publicity for the gospel," as Havner described it. Literally thousands of newscasts and newspaper articles around the world have given our staff and students a platform to share about God's powerful work in this crisis.

Yet, the good news of what has happened at Union in recent weeks really is part of a larger story that reaches far beyond Union University. That larger story says that God still works in this world to save people in their specific situations of life. Make no mistake; God does not "hop to," like a genie from a magic lamp anytime we call on Him to act—He is God and we are not, after all. Yet, the fact that we cannot order Him does not mean that He does not order circumstances in the lives of His people. He cares about people and still works in their lives in specific, tangible ways, and the way that God works in the world now is directly related to the greatest way He has ever worked in this world—the work God did in and through the life, ministry, death, and resurrection of His Son, Jesus Christ. In Luke 4:18 Jesus uses a passage from Isaiah 61:1 to describe His ministry. He says He has been anointed by God the Father "to preach good news."

As the Gospels—the "Good News" books of the New Testament—show, Jesus' ministry culminated in His death and resurrection, which are portrayed not as an end but as the beginning of a greater story. Ray Stedman, in *God's Loving Word*, writes, "The resurrection is not only the Good News, it is the best news imaginable,"[2] because the resurrection shows both who Jesus is and that even sin and death are not obstacles for the work God wants to do in the lives of people.

If God can defeat death and completely forgive our sins, He can deal with any challenge in our lives—any addiction, troubled relationship, crisis, or need. He also can turn death and destruction inside out for life and good. In other words, it is through Jesus that people can know God and experience life that is extraordinary. Yet, to know that life, we have to come to a realization that Jesus Christ really is Lord (or "Boss") of all that is and submit ourselves to His loving, wise rule of our lives.

That really is the back story behind the "tornado story" at Union University. The miracle of God's protection and His people's response had been in the making years before the tornado hit our campus. Certainly lives were changed that night, but as you can see from the stories in this book, these lives had already been deeply touched and changed by a profound relationship with God through Jesus.

At our university we spend a great deal of time discussing how to integrate our Christian faith—a truly Christian view of the world—with all aspects of life and learning. If Jesus really is Lord, then He knows more than anyone about math and music, physics and physical education, literature and languages, as well as marriage, parenting, and a host of other practical areas in modern life. Our community was able to respond the way it did to the tornado crisis because we already were thinking about various aspects of what God says is true about life and walking with God as He walked with us through the storm. We are not a perfect community, of course, but we have a patient, loving God who is working in our midst and changing us for the better. That process of change began with our understanding the "good news."

When we could do nothing for ourselves, this loving, merciful God reached down to us through the person of Jesus Christ—God Himself in human flesh. Jesus lived the perfect life. He died on the cross, bearing in Himself the penalty from God that we deserved to pay for our sins. He rose from the dead on the third day, proving His divine identity and displaying His power over sin and death. All those who turn to Christ as Boss, trusting in the sacrifice He made for sins—to protect us from the storm of God's wrath—will be saved.

This is not about merely joining a church, becoming more moral, being confirmed, or becoming religious. Noted author Kevin Vanhoozer writes, "At the heart of Christianity, what we find is neither a philosophy nor a system of morality, but a gospel: good news,"[3] and that good news is all about relationship. The question is not whether you have joined a church or been confirmed. The question is whether you have a real relationship with God—do you love Him and want to please Him more than anything? The gospel is not primarily about avoiding hell or getting to heaven; it is about God, as His gift to us, bringing us back into a healthy relationship with Himself.

Yuko Maruyama, a Japanese organist working in Minneapolis, was once a devout Buddhist. Now, thanks to the music of J. S. Bach, she is a Christian. "Bach introduced me to God, Jesus, and Christianity," she told *Metro Lutheran*, a Twin Cities monthly. "When I play a fugue, I can feel Bach talking to God."

Dear reader, as you have read "the music" of the stories in this book, could you "feel" the interaction between God and His people? Is it possible that God wants to use these "songs," these stories, to introduce you "to God, Jesus, and Christianity"? How will you respond?

If you have yet to do so, I would encourage you to pray to God right now. Tell Him that you are turning away from living life for yourself and turning to Him as your Boss in life. Ask Him, on the basis of what Jesus has done on the cross, to forgive you for your sins and put you in right relationship with Himself. Then, find a Christian friend and a good church that can help you grow in your relationship with God. If you would like further information on how to live as Christ's follower, feel free to call or write:

Campus Ministries
Union University
1050 Union University Dr.
Jackson, TN 38305
(731) 668-1818
E-mail: campusministries@uu.edu

The only thing that would make our story more complete would be if you would join us in this incredible journey, that you would know God as your "hope," your "shelter," and your "eternal home." May you too know the God in the whirlwind.

## Notes

1. John Blanchard, *The Complete Gathered Gold: A Treasury of Quotations for Christians* (Evangelism Press, 2006).
2. Ray C. Stedman, "God's Loving Word," *Christianity Today*, vol. 38, no. 4.
3. Kevin Vanhoozer, "Experience the Drama," Trinity Magazine, spring 2006, 19–21.

# ACKNOWLEDGMENTS

M y deepest thanks to so many people who have assisted with this project. Craig Davis, David Dockery, Gene Fant, Mark Kahler, Carla Sanderson, Greg Thornbury, and Ray Van Neste were kind enough to read the book in its entirety and offer valuable insights. My wife Sarah and my mother, Sylvia Ellsworth, did the same. I also appreciate the input from Timmy Brister, Ben Dockery, George Guthrie, Amanda Johnson, Jacque Taylor, Kimberly Thornbury, and Will Hall. My father, Roger Ellsworth, and my brother, Marty Ellsworth, were also an encouragement to me throughout the process.

Christy Young and Katrina Parker did much of my transcription work, and their help was invaluable. I also greatly appreciate the prayers and support from my church family at Cornerstone Community Church.

The outstanding written accounts by Julie Boyer and Heather Martin provided much of the basis for the chapters about them.

Thanks for Morris Abernathy for his photography which is included in this book, Todd Mullins for his help with the graphics, and other members of Union's Office of University Communications who were a great encouragement.

My other colleagues at Union, especially Dr. Dockery, with whom I am honored to work on a daily basis, and the Union students, who make my job a pleasure, deserve my deepest gratitude.

Thanks also to Tom Walters, Kim Stanford, David Shepherd, Brad Waggoner, David Schrader, and the team at B&H Publishing Group for making this project a reality.

And a very special thank you to Daniel and Emmalee, who sacrificed their time with Dad while he was busy writing, and for my wife Sarah, who graciously tackled the extra work created by my absence at home. I love you all very much.

# UNION UNIVERSITY

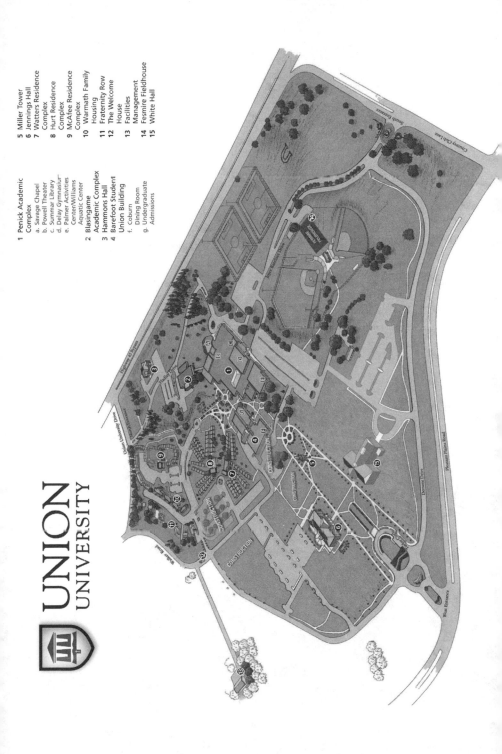

1 Penick Academic
   Complex
   a. Savage Chapel
   b. Powell Theater
   c. Summar Library
   d. Delay Gymnasium
   e. Palmer Activities
      Center/Williams
      Aquatic Center
2 Blasingame
   Academic Complex
3 Hammons Hall
4 Barefoot Student
   Union Building
   f. Coburn
      Dining Room
   g. Undergraduate
      Admissions

5 Miller Tower
6 Jennings Hall
7 Watters Residence
   Complex
8 Hurt Residence
   Complex
9 McAfee Residence
   Complex
10 Warmath Family
   Housing
11 Fraternity Row
12 The Welcome
   House
13 Facilities
   Management
14 Fesmire Fieldhouse
15 White Hall

7:02 p.m.

2.5.08

F-4 tornado

WE LOST BUILDINGS.
WE DIDN'T LOSE OUR *spirit.*

UNION
UNIVERSITY

DISASTER RELIEF FUND
731.661.5050  www.uurebuilding.com